Pray What

God Says

by

Christine Brooks Martin

Pray What God Says

ISBN: 978-0-692-01058-7

For information or to contact the author, write to:
CHRISTINE BROOKS MARTIN
5230 Clark Avenue, Suite 29
Lakewood, CA 90712

*Unless otherwise noted, all scripture references are from the King James
Version of the Bible.*

Printed in the USA by
Morris Publishing®
3212 E. Hwy 30
Kearney, NE 68847
800-650-7888
www.morrispublishing.com

TABLE OF CONTENTS

DEDICATIONS

"Pray What God Says" is dedicated to the memory of:
Bessie Pennington
John & Mae C. Brooks
Dollie Lee Martin
Mother Lavonia Verner
Bishop David Tillman
&
Ocie "Jeff" Jefferson

ACKNOWLEDGEMENTS

I thank my Lord and Saviour Jesus Christ for my sons, Fontay, Kevin and David; my grandchildren – Treveon, Javon, Jason, Sophia and Joshua. Chavilla, my daughter-in-law and prayer partner, you are precious to me, so thank you for our Naomi/Ruth relationship.

A special thank you to my best friends:

Cheryl Tillman-Lee, for praying and waiting 13 years in faith for me to say yes to salvation;

Dr. Daniel Horton, for your love, encouragement and the inspiration to write that chapter;

Sandrah Green, your wisdom and consolation kept me out of the corner;

And Edward Wilson, for always demonstrating joy in the high and low places.

I love you!:

To my mother, Annie Mae Straughter. Your sacrifice of years without me directed my path to Jesus, who brought us back to one another;

To Prosperity, my mentor and spiritual mother;

My first co-pastor Estella Tillman, who handed over the reins of Wednesday morning intercessory prayer to my charge;

Dorothy Daniels, thank you for introducing me to fasting, travailing prayer and shut-ins;

Apostle Dr. Robbie Horton, my pastor, for coaching and arming me for new realms and dimensions of faith;

Dr. Marea Channel, associate pastor, for your motivating grace;

To my trenches and prayer wall partners, Minister Daisy Martin-Bell, Prophetess Monique Hurd, Evangelist Charmaine E. Wright and Evangelist Sheryl Hamilton.

And to my church family at Anointed Connection (A.O.C.O.) International Ministries.

Dr. Garon Harden and Dr. Bettye Jean Harden of Greater Open Door C.O.G.I.C., I appreciate your tender love and wonderful instruction for my life upon my return to Los Angeles.

INTRODUCTION
Verily I say unto you, Whosoever shall not receive the kingdom of God as a little child, he shall not enter therein.
Mark 10:15

Just before my sixth birthday, my father passed away one evening while watching his favorite television program. In the days to follow, I was bewildered by my first encounter with death, then overwhelmed with fear that my mother would succumb as well after witnessing multiple fainting episodes and her inconsolable grief.

I slipped into the comfort of self-imposed silence and isolation. In the height of the day, I could be found sitting in the backyard swing pondering the whole situation while gazing at cloud formations. In the evening I staked out the sixth rung of the foyer staircase. From there I could peer into the living room and see my "sleeping" father. For two days he had been laid out for viewing at our home so family, friends, and co-workers could come to pay their last respects. I felt it was of benefit and necessity to maintain the vantage point from the stairs until bedtime in the event he was to awaken. I dared not miss what was inevitably unrequited expectation.

The day before dad's funeral, my mom's friend who we called Aunt Bessie decided to break my solitude by joining me in the backyard. She quietly watched me swing for what seemed like hours. Finally, I broke days of silence by asking her why my father could not wake up. I simply wanted him to wake up so mom would stop crying and we could be happy once again.

She said it was my father's time to go to a place called heaven and live with someone named Jesus Christ. And it was possible for everyone to do the same when it was their time to go, she added. Immediately, I thought of my grieving mother and worried about her leaving me all alone so she could join my father. But Aunt Bessie reassured me that it was not her time yet and she would eventually get better. The most comforting thing I heard however was that Jesus was taking care of my beloved father and this Jesus would be watching over me from heaven like a father, for the rest of my life.

Immediately, the floodgates burst open with many questions. I had a knack for intense interrogation (which my granddaughter has inherited). Aunt Bessie answered what she could sufficiently enough though, for me to become enamored with Jesus Christ. He could not be seen, she said, but I could talk to Him at any time.

Instantly my perplexities about death and fear for my mother's life, was gone and I could not explain the happiness that engulfed me. Although I missed my father and realized I would never experience his demonstrations of love for me again, I was no longer sad or afraid. My adolescent heart had experienced what I now know was inexplicable joy and peace.

I didn't know it at the time, but I had just been introduced to the tangibility of God and the rudimentary elements of prayer. With child-like faith I entered the gate of His kingdom by embracing the words I heard from His vessel of love, Aunt Bessie.

I grew into adulthood, living a self-pleasing life for most of it. But, it was in the living room of a dear friend (who eventually became my spiritual mother and mentor), that I was radically transformed. I was baptized by the Holy Spirit during a prayer accepting His salvation. An insatiable hunger to commune with God through His Word and times of prayer marked my new life.

As it is possible for anyone, through wisdom, knowledge and understanding garnered from the scriptures, prayer and life experiences, I have received the progressive inculcating, reality, benefits and power of prayer. The details of that process and progress would fill more journals than I could possibly write.

The intent of this guide however, is to reintroduce just one of many keys to effective prayer. That is simply to Pray What God Says. I have found that availing yourself to this prayer key can and will gain you access to a divine response. That response will yield a greater relationship with God the Father, through His Son Jesus Christ, with the enabling assistance of the Holy Spirit. It will yield the nourishing and strengthening of the spirit man; the release of blessing, healing and deliverance for yourself and those for whom you pray; and much more. The much more is the perpetual release of divine preparations that eyes have not seen, that ears have not heard, nor has entered into the heart of those who chose to love God. And my heart says Come Lord Jesus.

This once enamored child is continually maturing--through praying what God says--into a woman in love, heart, mind, soul and spirit, with my Heavenly Father.

CHAPTER 1: The Cry

For ye have not received the spirit of bondage again to fear;
but ye have received the Spirit of adoption,
whereby we cry, Abba, Father.
Romans 8:15

Throughout Genesis 1, as God was creating all things and man, He said it was good. We have yet to observe or experience every expression or facet of goodness and beauty that was designed by our Creator in the heavens, on and in the earth, or through the animate and inanimate.

God created man in His image. He formed man's body from the dust of the earth and breathed into him the breath of life. Man became a living soul with a God-given spirit, designed to be in direct and constant communion and relationship with his Creator.

Because of the fall of man in the Garden of Eden, we are all born with an Adamic (or sin) nature. Therefore, our soul is governed by the sensual realm. The soul is the mind, will and emotions. The five senses--see, hear, smell, touch and taste--influences and governs our soulish and behavioral responses. Our response to our senses are played out or evidenced through what we think, what we say and do, and how we feel.

There is an expression that says that the heart is the seat of the emotions. As our emotions are touched in various ways throughout life experiences, each one of us will express joy, hope, gratitude, affliction, fear, sickness, anger, disappointment, brokenness, etc. In concert with these expressions is a corresponding "cry" or sound from our spirit that will command or demand a response from something or someone greater than ourselves. God, who is the source of our spirit, desires that greater to be Himself.

Throughout the scriptures there are diverse ways this "cry" or sound is expressed.

1. To cry is to weep, shed tears, sob, bawl, whimper, whine, moan, groan, lament, grieve, mourn, or wail:
Because thine heart was tender, and thou didst humble thyself before God, when thou heardest his words against this place, and against the inhabitants thereof, and humbledst thyself before me, and

didst rend thy clothes, and weep before me; I have even heard thee also, saith the LORD. 2 Chronicles 34:27

Hear my prayer, O LORD, and give ear unto my cry; hold not thy peace at my tears: for I am a stranger with thee, and a sojourner, as all my fathers were. Psalm 39:12

For we that are in this tabernacle do groan, being burdened: not for that we would be unclothed, but clothed upon, that mortality might be swallowed up of life. 2 Corinthians 5:4

Verily, verily, I say unto you, That ye shall weep and lament, but the world shall rejoice: and ye shall be sorrowful, but your sorrow shall be turned into joy. John 16:20

Have mercy upon me, O LORD, for I am in trouble: mine eye is consumed with grief, yea, my soul and my belly. Psalm 31:9

Like a crane or a swallow, so did I chatter: I did mourn as a dove: mine eyes fail with looking upward: O LORD, I am oppressed; undertake for me. Isaiah 38:14

2. To cry does not have to be caused by sadness or negative feelings as in the previous examples of scripture. It also means to sing out, or praise with joy or excitement:

And He said, It is not the voice of them that shout for mastery, neither is it the voice of them that cry for being overcome: but the noise of them that sing do I hear. Exodus 32:18

And she conceived again, and bare a son: and she said, Now will I praise the LORD: therefore she called his name Judah; and left bearing. Genesis 29:35

Praise our God, all ye his servants, and ye that fear him, both small and great. Revelations 19:5

Also that day they offered great sacrifices, and rejoiced: for God had made them rejoice with great joy: the wives also and the children rejoiced: so that the joy of Jerusalem was heard even afar off. Nehemiah 12:43

But let all those that put their trust in thee rejoice: let them ever shout for joy, because thou defendest them: let them also that love thy name be joyful in thee. Psalm 5:11

And the disciples were filled with joy, and with the Holy Ghost. Act 13:52

4

3. To cry means to utter with spontaneous expression:
When Mordecai perceived all that was done, Mordecai rent his clothes, and put on sackcloth with ashes, and went out into the midst of the city, and cried with a loud and a bitter cry; Esther 4:1
Then Joseph could not refrain himself before all them that stood by him; and He cried. Cause every man to go out from me. And there stood no man with him, while Joseph made himself known unto his brethren. And He wept aloud: and the Egyptians and the house of Pharaoh heard. And Joseph said unto his brethren, I am Joseph; doth my father yet live? And his brethren could not answer him; for they were troubled at his presence. Genesis 45:1-3

4. To cry means to proclaim, announce, shout, to mobilize or motivate:
And ye shall hallow the fiftieth year, and proclaim liberty throughout all the land unto all the inhabitants thereof: it shall be a jubilee unto you; and ye shall return every man unto his possession, and ye shall return every man unto his family. Leviticus 25:10
Go and proclaim these words toward the north, and say, Return, thou backsliding Israel, saith the LORD; and I will not cause mine anger to fall upon you: for I am merciful, saith the LORD, and I will not keep anger for ever. Jeremiah 3:12

5. To cry means to call out or call to:
The righteous call to God--
A Psalm of David. Unto thee will I cry, O LORD my rock; be not silent to me: lest, if thou be silent to me, I become like them that go down into the pit. Hear the voice of my supplications, when I cry unto thee, when I lift up my hands toward thy holy oracle. Psalm 28:1-2
I will cry unto God most high; unto God that performeth all things for me. Psalm 57:2
By reason of the multitude of oppressions they make the oppressed to cry: they cry out by reason of the arm of the mighty. Job 35:9

Even wicked people cry out but to other gods--
Yet ye have forsaken me, and served other gods: wherefore I will deliver you no more. Go and cry unto the gods which ye have chosen; let them deliver you in the time of your tribulation. Judges 10:13-14

The Word says that everything created cries out--
Such as animals (beast):
And the wild beasts of the islands shall cry in their desolate houses, and dragons in their pleasant palaces: and her time is near to come, and her days shall not be prolonged. Isaiah 13:22
He giveth to the beast his food, and to the young ravens which cry. Psalm 147:9
The beasts of the field cry also unto thee: for the rivers of waters are dried up, and the fire hath devoured the pastures of the wilderness. Joel 1:20
But let man and beast be covered with sackcloth, and cry mightily unto God: yea, let them turn every one from his evil way, and from the violence that is in their hands. Jonah 3:8

Inanimate things cry out:
And He answered and said unto them, I tell you that, if these should hold their peace, the stones would immediately cry out. Luke 19:40

Devils and unclean spirits cry out:
And devils also came out of many, crying out, and saying, Thou art Christ the Son of God. And He rebuking them suffered them not to speak: for they knew that He was Christ. Luke 4:41
For unclean spirits, crying with loud voice, came out of many that were possessed with them: and many taken with palsies, and that were lame, were healed. Acts 8:7

Cities cry out:
And the LORD said, Because the cry of Sodom and Gomorrah is great, and because their sin is very grievous; I will go down now, and see whether they have done altogether according to the cry of it, which is come unto me; and if not, I will know. Genesis 18:20-21.
And the men that died not were smitten with the emerods: and the cry of the city went up to heaven. 1 Samuel 5:12

Even virtue cries out:
Doth not wisdom cry? and understanding put forth her voice? Proverbs 8:1

6. There is a cry in supplication for an immediate need, to implore, beg, plead, beseech, solicit, or entreat:

If, when evil cometh upon us, as the sword, judgment, or pestilence, or famine, we stand before this house, and in thy presence, for thy name is in this house, and cry unto thee in our affliction, then thou wilt hear and help. 2 Chronicles 20:9

And He said, I beseech thee, shew me thy glory. Exodus 33:18

I beseech thee, O LORD, remember now how I have walked before thee in truth and with a perfect heart, and have done that which is good in thy sight. And Hezekiah wept sore. 2 Kings 20:3

O Lord, I beseech thee, let now thine ear be attentive to the prayer of thy servant, and to the prayer of thy servants, who desire to fear thy name: and prosper, I pray thee, thy servant this day, and grant him mercy in the sight of this man. For I was the king's cupbearer. Nehemiah 1:11

Plead my cause, and deliver me: quicken me according to thy word. Psalm 119:154

7. The cry of intercession is a request on behalf of others, to travail or appeal:

He shall see of the travail of his soul, and shall be satisfied: by his knowledge shall my righteous servant justify many; for He shall bear their iniquities. Isaiah 53:11

For there shall be a day, that the watchmen upon the mount Ephraim shall cry, Arise ye, and let us go up to Zion unto the LORD our God. Jeremiah 31:6

And prayed unto him: and He was intreated of him, and heard his supplication, and brought him again to Jerusalem into his kingdom. Then Manasseh knew that the LORD He was God. 2 Chronicles 33:13

That thine eyes may be open unto the supplication of thy servant, and unto the supplication of thy people Israel, to hearken unto them in all that they call for unto thee. 1 Kings 8:52

But if they be prophets, and if the word of the LORD be with them, let them now make intercession to the LORD of hosts, that the vessels which are left in the house of the LORD, and in the house of the king of Judah, and at Jerusalem, go not to Babylon. Jeremiah 27:18

Wherefore He is able also to save them to the uttermost that come unto God by him, seeing He ever liveth to make intercession for them. Hebrews 7:25

By nature and divine design every human being has a heart cry or sound. As a believer--believing in your heart, accepting the redemptive work of Jesus Christ and confessing Him as Lord and Saviour—your regenerated spirit cries out for appeasement or fulfillment from God. Even an unsaved person has a heart cry. While exercising the liberty of free-will that God has given to all of us, a carnal-minded (or earthbound) person is self-assertive, self-gratifying, and self-willed. He has a tendency to not desire or submit to the spirit of God. The spirit of God and the Word of God finds no place in his thoughts, emotions, speech or decisions and choices. Instead they will defer to sensual or carnal ideologies, pleasures, solutions and remedies.

Years ago, before accepting Jesus Christ as Lord of my life, I considered myself a decent person. Although I acknowledged God, I did not serve Him by reading or studying the scriptures, prayer or attending church. I thought I had everything that was essential for a good and happy lifestyle. But I had issues that troubled my mind and heart as well. With God excluded from my life, unfruitful decisions made solutions to my problems elusive. I resigned to accepting and responding to lingering challenges the way I thought best.

But God heard the cry of my heart when no one else was listening, and where no one else was looking. He reconnected me with a friend in a wonderful way. My best friend Cheryl sowed 13 years of obedient and dedicated evangelistic ministry into my life. She planted the seed of the Word in every conversation and watered it by taking me to church services, conferences, her family gatherings, and most important, intercession for me in her prayer closet. I believe that when the Lord heard my cry for something new, He heard and honored the cries of Cheryl's heart to see me saved and filled with the Holy Spirit.

Throughout those 13 years I had many opportunities to accept an altar call but I refused, holding on to the notion that eventually, I could fix me all by myself. In retrospect, arrogance and stubbornness had been a barrier to my deliverance from the problems in my life.

On August 5, 1992, Cheryl needed to pick up some documents from an evangelist in Moreno Valley so I agreed to accompany her so she could use the Express lane. As we stepped into Evangelist Prosperity's living room, I immediately felt very hot. It was as if someone was pouring hot liquid on my head. Although the air conditioner was on in her home, I rationalized that my body was adjusting to coming in from the very warm temperature outside. So I sat quietly to cool off. After a few minutes Evangelist Prosperity glanced at me and asked if I was saved. I said, "No." Then she asked if I wanted to accept Jesus Christ as my personal Saviour. Without hesitation I replied, "Yes. Sure why not?"

As the three of us joined hands and Evangelist Prosperity began to pray for me, I felt the heat on my head intensify to what seemed like a thick liquid pouring from my head and neck, down to my feet. My heart raced, my legs felt too limp to stand. I thought I was having a heart attack or some other physical malady. I tried to tell them to call 911 but I couldn't speak English. With tears streaming down my face, peace and joy enveloped my very being and my lips stammered in tongues for nearly an hour.

Cheryl fell to her knees weeping and praising the Lord because she was able to witness the fruit of her labor from the prayers, and the planting and watering of the Word into my life. To some it would seem that I had a radical conversion experience. But I would never trade it for anything else because that experience has kept me believing, knowing and trusting that God is real and He loves me.

In my introduction to this book, I reflected on the peace and joy I experienced when I first heard about Jesus Christ from Aunt Bessie. But when I decided to accept Him as my Lord and Saviour in 1992, that same peace and joy embraced me but in a greater measure. I am fully persuaded that God's plan and purpose for my life is greater than I or anyone else could have fashioned it.

Since that day, I have learned that as you commit your life to Jesus Christ and receive the infilling of the Holy Spirit, there is a divine enablement to begin, build and establish a relationship with God. It is only through a relationship with Him, through learning the scriptures and prayer, that you will be able to live a regenerated life. This is a life that can be conformed and transformed daily to the likeness of Jesus Christ.

When my heart was crying out, I was not aware that it was directed toward God. There is a cry of our heart and it is of a hungry, thirsty spirit man crying out to his Creator. Even in death, the word says that the spirit of man returns to the Creator, our God. *Then shall the dust return to the earth as it was: and the spirit shall return unto God who gave it.* Ecclesiastes 12:7.

If we consistently allow the cry of our heart be directed toward the Lord, we are better able to submit our soul (mind, will and emotions) to His spirit. We have to allow ourselves to be subject to, in daily reliance upon, and in compliance with God and His holy scriptures. Commitment to desiring our thoughts and behavior to be in consistent alignment with the Holy Spirit will yield a lifestyle led by a spirit man that is in deference to holiness and righteousness. *This I say then, walk in the Spirit, and ye shall not fulfill the lust of the flesh.* Galatians 5:16.

God created and enables our hearts to cry out to Him: *And because ye are sons, God hath sent forth the Spirit of his Son into your hearts, crying, Abba, Father.* Galatians 4:6.

He hears and is attentive to the cry of our heart: *Lord, hear my voice: let thine ears be attentive to the voice of my supplications.* Psalm 130:2.

He responds to the cry of our heart and causes it to be filled with joy and gladness: *But be ye glad and rejoice for ever in that which I create: for, behold, I create Jerusalem a rejoicing, and her people a joy.* Isaiah 65:18.

He is a defender for the cry of the heart that seeks protection and justice: *And shall not God avenge his own elect, which cry day and night unto him, though He bear long with them?* Luke 18:7.

God has an ultimate plan for every cry of the heart: *And God shall wipe away all tears from their eyes; and there shall be no more death, neither sorrow, nor crying, neither shall there be any more pain: for the former things are passed away.* Revelations 21:4.

The cry of every man's heart is for provision, protection, health and well being. We require direction, revelation, truth, justice and more. There is nothing or anyone better to turn to than the Creator of all things, the Lord our Maker. He has made a covenant--His Word--that guarantees that He is the one who can provide His joy, peace, protection, His provision, plan, solution and elevation to our life.

If you have not accepted Jesus Christ as your Lord you can do so now. Say the following and mean it from your heart.

Father, your Word says that sin separates us from you. But when Jesus Christ was put on the cross, He bore the sin of the world. The shedding of His blood was the perfect sacrifice necessary to redeem all mankind from the consequences of sin and that sacrifice brought us into right relationship with you. So now, I confess that I am a sinner. I believe that Jesus died for all my sin. I repent of my sin. I renounce and am willing to forsake a life of sin. I ask you to forgive me. I believe in my heart that you have removed sin far from me and put it on the cross. I believe that by your power, you raised Jesus from the dead and He is now Lord over sin and death. As I give my heart to Jesus, I confess Him as my Lord and that I am a new creature. Old things have passed away and all things are become new. Each day, I will place my hope, trust, needs and expectations in You in the name of Jesus.

When you receive Jesus, you have accepted what He has done for you on the cross. You are redeemed and have become a child of God for all eternity.

As many as received him, to them He gave the right to become children of God, even to those who believe in His name. John 1:12

CHAPTER 2: The Lie

...A Psalm of David. The fool hath said in his heart,
There is no God. They are corrupt, they have done
abominable works, there is none that doeth good.
The LORD looked down from heaven upon the children of men,
to see if there were any that did understand, and seek God.
Psalm 14:1-2

The lies of satan are many. To follow are some we hear most often. I choose to allow what the scriptures have to say be my opinion of the truth.

1. Lie: There is no God.

The truth according to the Word of God:

But the LORD is the true God, he is the living God, and an everlasting king: at his wrath the earth shall tremble, and the nations shall not be able to abide his indignation. Jeremiah 10:10

For they themselves shew of us what manner of entering in we had unto you, and how ye turned to God from idols to serve the living and true God; 1 Timothy 1:9

For therefore we both labour and suffer reproach, because we trust in the living God, who is the Saviour of all men, specially of those that believe. 1 Timothy 4:10

2. Lie: There is no hell.

The truth according to the Word of God:

And many shall follow their pernicious ways; by reason of whom the way of truth shall be evil spoken of. And through covetousness shall they with feigned words make merchandise of you: whose judgment now of a long time lingereth not, and their damnation slumbereth not. For if God spared not the angels that sinned, but cast them down to hell, and delivered them into chains of darkness, to be reserved unto judgment; And spared not the old world, but saved Noah the eighth person, a preacher of righteousness, bringing in the flood upon the world of the ungodly; And turning the cities of Sodom and Gomorrha into ashes condemned them with an overthrow, making them an ensample unto those that after should live ungodly; 2 Peter 2:2-6

I am he that liveth, and was dead; and, behold, I am alive for evermore, Amen; and have the keys of hell and of death. Revelations 1:18

3. Lie: You are the only one going through what you're going through.

The truth according to the Word of God:

And I will come down and talk with thee there: and I will take of the spirit which is upon thee, and will put it upon them; and they shall bear the burden of the people with thee, that thou bear it not thyself alone. Numbers 11:17

We then that are strong ought to bear the infirmities of the weak, and not to please ourselves. Romans 15:1

4. Lie: Your circumstance is greater than you can bear.

The truth according to the Word of God:

I will not leave you comfortless: I will come to you. John 14:18

There hath no temptation taken you but such as is common to man: but God is faithful, who will not suffer you to be tempted above that ye are able; but will with the temptation also make a way to escape, that ye may be able to bear it. 1 Corinthians 10:13

5. Lie: God does not care about you.

The truth according to the Word of God:

Let your conversation be without covetousness; and be content with such things as ye have: for he hath said, I will never leave thee, nor forsake thee. Hebrews 13:5

And ye shall be holy unto me: for I the LORD am holy, and have severed you from other people, that ye should be mine. Leviticus 20:26

That they may walk in my statutes, and keep mine ordinances, and do them: and they shall be my people, and I will be their God. Ezekiel 11:20

6. Lie: You can get to Heaven with good works and without Jesus.

The truth according to the Word of God:

Whosoever shall confess that Jesus is the Son of God, God dwelleth in him, and he in God. 1 John 4:15

No man can come to me, except the Father which hath sent me draw him: and I will raise him up at the last day. John 6:44

That if thou shalt confess with thy mouth the Lord Jesus, and shalt believe in thine heart that God hath raised him from the dead, thou shalt be saved. Romans 10:9

7. Lie: The Bible is just a book written by men.
The truth according to the Word of God:
All scripture is given by inspiration of God, and is profitable for doctrine, for reproof, for correction, for instruction in righteousness: 2 Timothy 3:16

8. Lie: Jesus was only a prophet.
The truth according to the Word of God:
And devils also came out of many, crying out, and saying, Thou art Christ the Son of God. And he rebuking them suffered them not to speak: for they knew that he was Christ. Luke 4:41
Unto you first God, having raised up his Son Jesus, sent him to bless you, in turning away every one of you from his iniquities. Acts 3:26

9. Lie: There are no miracles for the New Testament church.
The truth according to the Word of God:
Now ye are the body of Christ, and members in particular. And God hath set some in the church, first apostles, secondarily prophets, thirdly teachers, after that miracles, then gifts of healings, helps, governments, diversities of tongues. 1 Corinthians 12:27-28

10. Lie: It's OK to worship any god.
The truth according to the Word of God:
For all the gods of the nations are idols: but the LORD made the heavens. Psalm 96:5
The LORD will be terrible unto them: for he will famish all the gods of the earth; and men shall worship him, every one from his place, even all the isles of the heathen. Zephaniah 2:11
They have set up kings, but not by me: they have made princes, and I knew it not: of their silver and their gold have they made them idols, that they may be cut off. Hosea 8:4
And what agreement hath the temple of God with idols? for ye are the temple of the living God; as God hath said, I will dwell in them, and walk in them; and I will be their God, and they shall be my people. 2 Corinthians 6:16

The scriptures have much to say about lies and liars:

Wherefore hear the word of the LORD, ye scornful men, that rule this people which is in Jerusalem. Because ye have said, We have made a covenant with death, and with hell are we at agreement; when the overflowing scourge shall pass through, it shall not come unto us: for we have made lies our refuge, and under falsehood have we hid ourselves: Isaiah 28:14-15

Oh that I had in the wilderness a lodging place of wayfaring men; that I might leave my people, and go from them! for they be all adulterers, an assembly of treacherous men. And they bend their tongues like their bow for lies: but they are not valiant for the truth upon the earth; for they proceed from evil to evil, and they know not me, saith the LORD. Take ye heed every one of his neighbour, and trust ye not in any brother: for every brother will utterly supplant, and every neighbour will walk with slanders. And they will deceive every one his neighbour, and will not speak the truth: they have taught their tongue to speak lies, and weary themselves to commit iniquity. Thine habitation is in the midst of deceit; through deceit they refuse to know me, saith the LORD. Jeremiah 9:2-6

What are lies and who are liars?

1. Lies are false, untrue, evasive, exaggeration, and misrepresentation.

A faithful witness will not lie: but a false witness will utter lies. Proverb 14:5

Now the Spirit speaketh expressly, that in the latter times some shall depart from the faith, giving heed to seducing spirits, and doctrines of devils; Speaking lies in hypocrisy; having their conscience seared with a hot iron; 1 Timothy 4:1-2

2. Lies are perversion, distortion, corruption, slanted and twisted.

For the idols have spoken vanity, and the diviners have seen a lie, and have told false dreams; they comfort in vain: therefore they went their way as a flock, they were troubled, because there was no shepherd. Zechariah 10:2

And changed the glory of the uncorruptible God into an image made like to corruptible man, and to birds, and four-footed beasts, and creeping things. Wherefore God also gave them up to uncleanness through the lusts of their own hearts, to dishonour their own bodies

between themselves: Who changed the truth of God into a lie, and worshipped and served the creature more than the Creator, who is blessed for ever. Amen. Romans 1:23-25
But chiefly them that walk after the flesh in the lust of uncleanness, and despise government. Presumptuous are they, selfwilled, they are not afraid to speak evil of dignities. Whereas angels, which are greater in power and might, bring not railing accusation against them before the Lord. But these, as natural brute beasts, made to be taken and destroyed, speak evil of the things that they understand not; and shall utterly perish in their own corruption; And shall receive the reward of unrighteousness, as they that count it pleasure to riot in the day time. Spots they are and blemishes, sporting themselves with their own deceivings while they feast with you; Having eyes full of adultery, and that cannot cease from sin; beguiling unstable souls: an heart they have exercised with covetous practices; cursed children: Which have forsaken the right way, and are gone astray, following the way of Balaam the son of Bosor, who loved the wages of unrighteousness 2 Peter 2:10-15

3. Lies are inaccuracy, misconstruction, and contradiction.
Love not the world, neither the things that are in the world. If any man love the world, the love of the Father is not in him. For all that is in the world, the lust of the flesh, and the lust of the eyes, and the pride of life, is not of the Father, but is of the world. And the world passeth away, and the lust thereof: but he that doeth the will of God abideth for ever. 1 John 2:15-17

4. A lie is a rumor, hoax, forgery, a counterfeit, it is shameless, defamation, and fake.
If we say that we have fellowship with him, and walk in darkness, we lie, and do not the truth: 1 John 1:6
Now the Spirit speaketh expressly, that in the latter times some shall depart from the faith, giving heed to seducing spirits, and doctrines of devils; Speaking lies in hypocrisy; having their conscience seared with a hot iron; 1 Timothy 4:1-2

5. Liars deny, dispute, challenge, rebut, negate, or attempt to overthrow.

The proud have forged a lie against me: but I will keep thy precepts with my whole heart. Psalm 119:69

The wicked are estranged from the womb: they go astray as soon as they be born, speaking lies. Psalm 58:3

But there were false prophets also among the people, even as there shall be false teachers among you, who privily shall bring in damnable heresies, even denying the Lord that bought them, and bring upon themselves swift destruction. And many shall follow their pernicious ways; by reason of whom the way of truth shall be evil spoken of. And through covetousness shall they with feigned words make merchandise of you: whose judgment now of a long time lingereth not, and their damnation slumbereth not. 2 Peter 2:1-3

6. Liars mislead, deceive, or misinform.

If a man walking in the spirit and falsehood do lie, saying, I will prophesy unto thee of wine and of strong drink; he shall even be the prophet of this people. Micah 2:11

And thou, Pashur, and all that dwell in thine house shall go into captivity: and thou shalt come to Babylon, and there thou shalt die, and shalt be buried there, thou, and all thy friends, to whom thou hast prophesied lies. Jeremiah 20:6

Thus saith the LORD; For three transgressions of Judah, and for four, I will not turn away the punishment thereof; because they have despised the law of the LORD, and have not kept his commandments, and their lies caused them to err, after the which their fathers have walked: Amos 2:4

For the idols have spoken vanity, and the diviners have seen a lie, and have told false dreams; they comfort in vain: therefore they went their way as a flock, they were troubled, because there was no shepherd. Zechariah 10:2

God has made a provision for His creation. It is the words of His holy scriptures. When we choose to read, hear, learn and speak the Word of God it is able to save us, deliver us, and protect us from lies and liars.

CHAPTER 3: The Truth

*But the anointing which ye have received of him abideth in you,
and ye need not that any man teach you: but as the same anointing
teacheth you of all things, and is truth, and is no lie,
and even as it hath taught you, ye shall abide in him.*
1 John 2:27

Truth is defined as integrity, righteousness, sincerity, veracity, accuracy, just and authentic. The Holy Spirit is the spirit of truth. When you received Jesus Christ as your Lord and Saviour, and the indwelling presence of the Holy Spirit, you became the temple and tabernacle of God. The spirit of truth dwells IN you and is opposed to falsehood, lies or deceit. The Holy Spirit reveals truth as you study to understand and know God through the scriptures and relationship with Him through prayer. His truth is found in the scriptures and the scriptures are truth.

And the LORD passed by before him, and proclaimed, The LORD, The LORD God, merciful and gracious, longsuffering, and abundant in goodness and truth, Exodus 34:6

In hope of eternal life, which God, that cannot lie, promised before the world began; Titus 1:2

That by two immutable things, in which it was impossible for God to lie, we might have a strong consolation, who have fled for refuge to lay hold upon the hope set before us: Hebrews 6:18

He that speaketh truth sheweth forth righteousness: but a false witness deceit. Proverbs 12:17

For the fruit of the Spirit is in all goodness and righteousness and truth; Ephesian 5:9

But we are bound to give thanks alway to God for you, brethren beloved of the Lord, because God hath from the beginning chosen you to salvation through sanctification of the Spirit and belief of the truth: 2 Thessalonians 2:13

And hereby we know that we are of the truth, and shall assure our hearts before him. 1 John 3:19

For I rejoiced greatly, when the brethren came and testified of the truth that is in thee, even as thou walkest in the truth. 3 John 1:3

2. The spirit of truth is reality, factual, genuine, sound, valid, certain, upright and credible. The Holy Spirit of God is WITH you and is opposed to hypocrisy, pretense, deception, custom or over-inflation.

Let us draw near with a true heart in full assurance of faith, having our hearts sprinkled from an evil conscience, and our bodies washed with pure water. Hebrews 10:22
   I have chosen the way of truth: thy judgments have I laid before me. Psalm 119:30
   Thy righteousness is an everlasting righteousness, and thy law is the truth. Psalm 119:142
   For the law was given by Moses, but grace and truth came by Jesus Christ. John 1:17
   Who will have all men to be saved, and to come unto the knowledge of the truth. 1 Timothy 2:4

3. The spirit of truth is inside information, closeness, openness, liberal and believable.
   The Holy Spirit of God HEARS you and will answer.

And this is the record, that God hath given to us eternal life, and this life is in his Son. He that hath the Son hath life; and he that hath not the Son of God hath not life. These things have I written unto you that believe on the name of the Son of God; that ye may know that ye have eternal life, and that ye may believe on the name of the Son of God. 1 John 5:11-13
   For this is good and acceptable in the sight of God our Saviour; Who will have all men to be saved, and to come unto the knowledge of the truth. 1 Timothy 2:3-4
   The eyes of the LORD are upon the righteous, and his ears are open unto their cry. Psalm 34:15
   He will fulfill the desire of them that fear him: he also will hear their cry, and will save them. Psalm 145:19
   For the people shall dwell in Zion at Jerusalem: thou shalt weep no more: he will be very gracious unto thee at the voice of thy cry; when he shall hear it, he will answer thee. Isaiah 30:19
   And shall not God avenge his own elect, which cry day and night unto him, though he bear long with them? Luke 18:7

4. The spirit of truth is faithful, honest, honorable, candor, and frank. The Holy Spirit of God HELPS you and answers with fidelity, sincerity and punctuality in keeping promise, mercy and kindness.

For the vision is yet for an appointed time, but at the end it shall speak, and not lie: though it tarry, wait for it; because it will surely come, it will not tarry. Habbakuk 2:3
All the paths of the LORD are mercy and truth unto such as keep his covenant and his testimonies. Psalm 25:10
And ye shall know the truth, and the truth shall make you free. John 8:32
Jesus saith unto him, I am the way, the truth, and the life: no man cometh unto the Father, but by me. John 14:6
Pilate therefore said unto him, Art thou a king then? Jesus answered, Thou sayest that I am a king. To this end was I born, and for this cause came I into the world, that I should bear witness unto the truth. Every one that is of the truth heareth my voice. John 18:37
Wherefore I will not be negligent to put you always in remembrance of these things, though ye know them, and be established in the present truth. 2 Peter 1:12
But the hour cometh, and now is, when the true worshippers shall worship the Father in spirit and in truth: for the Father seeketh such to worship him. God is a Spirit: and they that worship him must worship him in spirit and in truth.
John 4:23-24

5. The spirit of truth is strictness, a principle, rule, law and precept. The Holy Spirit of God PROTECTS you with the true doctrine of the gospel.

O foolish Galatians, who hath bewitched you, that ye should not obey the truth, before whose eyes Jesus Christ hath been evidently set forth, crucified among you? This only would I learn of you, Received ye the Spirit by the works of the law, or by the hearing of faith? Are ye so foolish? having begun in the Spirit, are ye now made perfect by the flesh? Have ye suffered so many things in vain? if it be yet in vain. He therefore that ministereth to you the Spirit, and worketh miracles among you, doeth he it by the works of the law, or by the hearing of faith? Galatians 3:1-5

Happy is he that hath the God of Jacob for his help, whose hope is in the LORD his God: Which made heaven, and earth, the sea, and all that therein is: which keepeth truth for ever: Psalm 146:5-6

Stand therefore, having your loins girt about with truth, and having on the breastplate of righteousness; Ephesians 6:14

Seeing ye have purified your souls in obeying the truth through the Spirit unto unfeigned love of the brethren, see that ye love one another with a pure heart fervently: 1 Peter 1:2

CHAPTER 4: The Word

In the beginning was the Word, and the Word was
with God, and the Word was God.
John 1:1

The truth is the Word of God. The Word is the will and plan of God and is of God. The God-inspired written Word is called His holy scriptures. The scriptures give us history and the revelation of the future of God's creation. They are the voice of God revealing Himself to His creation and is the basis and foundation of God's power. It is the manual that outlines His plan for man's individual and collective purpose and destiny.

By studying the scriptures you discover God's character and virtue, and the will (covenant or provisional promises) He has given to every believer. You have an opportunity to learn, know and understand His authority and the authority you have in the name of Jesus Christ. Through a consistent dependence on the Holy Spirit to assist you in developing your relationship with God, you gain wisdom, knowledge and understanding of the scriptures, and will discover what His expectations are of you and what you can expect from Him.

The degree or level of the Word that abides in you, plus your faith, plus sincere desire, plus the confession that comes out of your mouth can equal the degree or level of what you can expect to manifest in your life. *Now unto him that is able to do exceeding abundantly above all that we ask or think, according to the power that worketh in us,* Ephesians 3:20.

By studying the scriptures you find out what the Word of God is TO YOU. It is: *perfect, pure, sure, right, nigh thee, established, made flesh, sent by God, salvation, faithful, the seed, testimony, sword of the spirit, quick, powerful, good, settled, a lamp, a light, it is true and reveals the truth, it is life, a flaming fire, deliverance, life, healing, spirit, sweet, unlimited, operative, eternal, divine strength or ability, effective, a discerner* (cuts out the unnecessary, adds what is needed, determines if you have the nature of God and walking out the purposes of God), *it is alive, the covenant, a promise, precept, statute, command, and the law.*

You also find out what the Word of God DOES FOR YOU. The sovereign work of God through the Holy Spirit: *Converts the soul, making the simple wise, rejoices the heart, enlightens the eyes, rewards, purifies, redeems, reconciles us to God, motivates, causes us to rest in the law, boasts of God, approves excellent things, is a light to those walking in darkness, instructs the foolish, is a teacher of babes, causes us to walk in godliness, judges, cleanses, consecrates, makes us obedient, purges, refines, causes you to overcome, increases, sanctifies, redeems, abides in us, heals, opposes sin, runneth very swiftly, gives understanding, delivers, is magnified, gives peace, performs, goes forth out of His mouth, warns, hastens, stands forever, is never broken, leads, humbles, keeps us, talks, reproves, instructs, is sent, directs, rains. It is fulfilled/manifested, executed, it casts out spirits, does not pass away/eternal, leads us to Christ, quickens, establishes, settles you, reveals God and our need for and dependence on Christ, reveals God's character, will and authority, gives wisdom, knowledge, understanding, council and revelation, helps you reverence God, translates you, propels you, accelerates you, makes you not ashamed. There is no condemnation to those who are in Christ, opens the eyes, ears, transforms, renews, and it restores.*

You find out WHO YOU ARE in the Word.

You have been redeemed, bought with a price with His precious blood: *For ye are bought with a price: therefore glorify God in your body, and in your spirit, which are God's.* 1 Corinthians 6:20.

Because of the Word of God you have been forgiven, made clean and reconciled to God: *For if, when we were enemies, we were reconciled to God by the death of his Son, much more, being reconciled, we shall be saved by his life.* Romans 5:10.

As a believer in Jesus Christ, you are able to cast out devils in His name: *And these signs shall follow them that believe; In my name shall they cast out devils; they shall speak with new tongues;* Mark 16:17.

You will also discover that you have been called and chosen according to God's purpose: *Who hath saved us, and called us with an holy calling, not according to our works, but according to his own purpose and grace, which was given us in Christ Jesus before the world began,* 2 Timothy 1:9.

You are a branch connected to the vine: *Abide in me, and I in you. As the branch cannot bear fruit of itself, except it abide in the vine; no more can ye, except ye abide in me.* John 15:4.

You are an epistle, a letter of Christ, not written with ink: *Forasmuch as ye are manifestly declared to be the epistle of Christ ministered by us, written not with ink, but with the Spirit of the living*

God; not in tables of stone, but in fleshy tables of the heart.
2 Corinthians 3:3.

The Word says that you are servants of God: *But now being made free from sin, and become servants to God, ye have your fruit unto holiness, and the end everlasting life.* Romans 6:22.

You are a part of the body of Christ: *Now ye are the body of Christ, and members in particular.* 1 Corinthians 12:27.

A peculiar people, aliens, ambassador, heavenly representative: *But ye are a chosen generation, a royal priesthood, an holy nation, a peculiar people; that ye should shew forth the praises of him who hath called you out of darkness into his marvellous light:* 1 Peter 2:9.

You are a bold witness for Christ: *But ye shall receive power, after that the Holy Ghost is come upon you: and ye shall be witnesses unto me both in Jerusalem, and in all Judaea, and in Samaria, and unto the uttermost part of the earth.* Act 1:8.

You are an heir of God and joint heir with Christ Jesus: *And if children, then heirs; heirs of God, and joint-heirs with Christ; if so be that we suffer with him, that we may be also glorified together.* Romans 8:17.

You are the salt of the earth: *Ye are the salt of the earth: but if the salt have lost his savour, wherewith shall it be salted? it is thenceforth good for nothing, but to be cast out, and to be trodden under foot of men.* Matthew 5:13

A king and priest: *And hast made us unto our God kings and priests: and we shall reign on the earth.* Revelations 5:10.

Isn't it great to know that you are blessed in the city and in the field?: *Blessed shalt thou be in the city, and blessed shalt thou be in the field.* Deuteronomy 28:3.

You are the head and not the tail, above and not beneath: *And the LORD shall make thee the head, and not the tail; and thou shalt be above only, and thou shalt not be beneath; if that thou hearken unto the commandments of the LORD thy God, which I command thee this day, to observe and to do them:* Deuteronomy 28:13.

You are rich in Him: *Hearken, my beloved brethren, Hath not God chosen the poor of this world rich in faith, and heirs of the kingdom which he hath promised to them that love him?* James 2:5.

Filled with the fruit of the spirit: *And be not drunk with wine, wherein is excess; but be filled with the Spirit;* Ephesians 5:18.

Baptized in the Holy Spirit: *And they were all filled with the Holy*

Ghost, and began to speak with other tongues, as the Spirit gave them utterance. Acts 2:4.

You are endued with power from on High: *And, behold, I send the promise of my Father upon you: but tarry ye in the city of Jerusalem, until ye be endued with power from on high.* Luke 24:49.

The Word says that you can overcome the wicked one and the world: *I write unto you, fathers, because ye have known him that is from the beginning. I write unto you, young men, because ye have overcome the wicked one. I write unto you, little children, because ye have known the Father.* 1 John 2:13.

And you are free from sin and death and the law of sickness, disease and captivity: *For the law of the Spirit of life in Christ Jesus hath made me free from the law of sin and death.* Romans 8:2.

The Word of God will affirm what you have, what you can do, and who you are in Christ Jesus.

We are to be mindful of God by:

Remembering the Word—*I will delight myself in thy statutes: I will not forget thy word.* Psalm 119:16.

But the mercy of the LORD is from everlasting to everlasting upon them that fear him, and his righteousness unto children's children; To such as keep his covenant, and to those that remember his commandments to do them. Psalm 103:17-18.

Learning the Word daily—*Take my yoke upon you, and learn of me; for I am meek and lowly in heart: and ye shall find rest unto your souls.* Matthews 11:29.

Seeking after God through the Word—*But without faith it is impossible to please him: for he that cometh to God must believe that he is, and that he is a rewarder of them that diligently seek him.* Hebrews 11:6.

Meditating in the Word—*My hands also will I lift up unto thy commandments, which I have loved; and I will meditate in thy statutes.* Psalm 119:48.

Getting an understanding of the Word—*Make me to understand the way of thy precepts: so shall I talk of thy wondrous works.* Psalm 119:27.

Considering the Word—*And all men shall fear, and shall declare the work of God; for they shall wisely consider of his doing.* Psalm 64:9.

Our ears are for hearing and is the gate of access to faith and a point of influence.

Use your ears to hear and be taught the Word—*It is written in the prophets, And they shall be all taught of God. Every man therefore that hath heard, and hath learned of the Father, cometh unto me.* John 6:45

Retain what you hear—*But he said, Yea rather, blessed are they that hear the word of God, and keep it.* Luke 11:28

Pay attention to what you hear for knowledge and understanding—*My son, attend unto my wisdom, and bow thine ear to my understanding:* Proverbs 5:1

Take heed and obey what you hear—*Take heed unto thyself, and unto the doctrine; continue in them: for in doing this thou shalt both save thyself, and them that hear thee.* 1 Timothy 4:16

Our eyes are the point of perception and observation.

Use your eyes to diligently seek truth and understanding from the Word of God—*But without faith it is impossible to please him: for he that cometh to God must believe that he is, and that he is a rewarder of them that diligently seek him.* Hebrews 11:6

Observe or pay attention to what you see—*Go ye therefore, and teach all nations, baptizing them in the name of the Father, and of the Son, and of the Holy Ghost: Teaching them to observe all things whatsoever I have commanded you: and, lo, I am with you alway, even unto the end of the world. Amen.* Matthew 28:19-20.

Our mouth is used for the outward expression of our heart and mind.

With every opportunity you should rejoice over the Word—*Glory ye in his holy name: let the heart of them rejoice that seek the LORD.* 1 Chronicles 16:10.

Use your mouth to speak the Word—*Which things also we speak, not in the words which man's wisdom teacheth, but which the Holy Ghost teacheth; comparing spiritual things with spiritual.* 1 Corinthians 2:13

Use your mouth to inquire or ask God questions about your life and concerns—*One thing have I desired of the LORD, that will I seek after; that I may dwell in the house of the LORD all the days of my life, to behold the beauty of the LORD, and to enquire in his temple.* Psalm 27:4

Praise the Lord with your mouth—*For both he that sanctifieth and they who are sanctified are all of one: for which cause he is not ashamed to call them brethren, Saying, I will declare thy name unto my brethren, in the midst of the church will I sing praise unto thee.* Hebrews 2:11-12

Preach or share the Word with others—*Preach the word; be instant in season, out of season; reprove, rebuke, exhort with all longsuffering and doctrine.* 2 Timothy 4:2

Tell about the redemptive work of Jesus to those who have not heard—*Go ye therefore, and teach all nations, baptizing them in the name of the Father, and of the Son, and of the Holy Ghost:* Matthew 28:19

Declare to yourself that the Word of God is truth and light—*This then is the message which we have heard of him, and declare unto you, that God is light, and in him is no darkness at all.* 1 John 1:5

Proclamations are seeds for the harvest of souls—*The Spirit of the Lord GOD is upon me; because the LORD hath anointed me to preach good tidings unto the meek; he hath sent me to bind up the brokenhearted, to proclaim liberty to the captives, and the opening of the prison to them that are bound;* Isaiah 61:1

Decree or apply the Word to every situation or circumstance—*Thou shalt also decree a thing, and it shall be established unto thee: and the light shall shine upon thy ways.* Job 22:28

Speaking what the Word says is appropriating the power of God—*If any man speak, let him speak as the oracles of God; if any man minister, let him do it as of the ability which God giveth: that God in all things may be glorified through Jesus Christ to whom be praise and dominion for ever and ever. Amen.* 1 Peter 4:11

What we take to heart rules and governs our emotions and affections. The Word of God should have priority over what is allowed to be a seed to take root in your heart.

Hide or guard the Word as you allow it to take an abiding place in your heart—*But we speak the wisdom of God in a mystery, even the hidden wisdom, which God ordained before the world unto our glory:* 1 Corinthians 2:7

Keep your hope in the truth—*Thou art my hiding place and my shield: I hope in thy word.* Psalm 119:114

Love and cherish the Word—*And this is love, that we walk after his commandments. This is the commandment, That, as ye have heard from the beginning, ye should walk in it.* 2 John 1:6

Keep or obey the Word—*But whoso keepeth his word, in him verily is the love of God perfected: hereby know we that we are in him.* 1 John 2:5

Trust in the Word—*For our exhortation was not of deceit, nor of uncleanness, nor in guile: But as we were allowed of God to be put in trust with the gospel, even so we speak; not as pleasing men, but God, which trieth our hearts.* 1 Thessalonians 2:3-4

Gladly and humbly receive the Word in every capacity (exhortation, correction, rebuke, admonition)—*Then they that gladly received his word were baptized: and the same day there were added unto them about three thousand souls.* Acts 2:41

Obey the Word with sincerity—*If they obey and serve him, they shall spend their days in prosperity, and their years in pleasures.* Job 36:11

Rejoice in the Word as a priceless, precious treasure—*I rejoice at thy word, as one that findeth great spoil.* Psalm 119:162

Choose to stand in awe of the Word because of the brilliance of it—*Let all the earth fear the LORD: let all the inhabitants of the world stand in awe of him.* Psalm 33:8

Do not forsake the truth—*Get wisdom, get understanding: forget it not; neither decline from the words of my mouth. Forsake her not, and she shall preserve thee: love her, and she shall keep thee.* Proverbs 4:5-6

Choose to know God through His Word—*And hereby we do know that we know him, if we keep his commandments.* 1 John 2:3

Believe the Word because it is truth—*For this cause also thank we God without ceasing, because, when ye received the word of God which ye heard of us, ye received it not as the word of men, but as it is in truth, the word of God, which effectually worketh also in you that believe.* 1 Thessalonians 2:13

Delight in the word—*But his delight is in the law of the LORD; and in his law doth he meditate day and night.* Psalm 1:2 We use our hands and feet for functional, practical application and activity.

Write out the scriptures, take notes during sermons and teaching sessions, take note of your revelation of the truth during personal study—*And the LORD answered me, and said, Write the vision, and make it plain upon tables, that he may run that readeth it.* Habakkuk 2:2

Do what the Word tells you to do—*And whatsoever we ask, we receive of him, because we keep his commandments, and do those things that are pleasing in his sight.* 1 John 3:22

Continue in (obey) and be reliable and consistent—*But continue thou in the things which thou hast learned and hast been assured of, knowing of whom thou hast learned them;* 2 Timothy 3:14

You can overcome challenge by walking in or activating the authority the Word has given you—*I have written unto you, fathers, because ye have known him that is from the beginning. I have written unto you, young men, because ye are strong, and the word of God abideth in you, and ye have overcome the wicked one.* 1 John 2:14

Let everything you put your hands to be done with excellence, integrity and diligence—*Every man also to whom God hath given riches and wealth, and hath given him power to eat thereof, and to take his portion, and to rejoice in his labour; this is the gift of God.* Ecclesiastes 5:19

Walk in or be a witness to others of what you know and believe of the word—*The LORD shall establish thee an holy people unto himself, as he hath sworn unto thee, if thou shalt keep the commandments of the LORD thy God, and walk in his ways.* Deuteronomy 28:9

Activating the Word of God in your life takes time and concerted effort. That effort is naturally and spiritually appropriating the scriptures to every facet of your being. As you study, meditate and learn to tap into God through His Word, He will tap into your life. Yielding and submitting to the transforming power of the scriptures and the Holy Spirit allows God to transition you for the greater. Alignment to His Word and its truth aligns you for kingdom experiences where you will have revelation of your assignments, God's plan and purpose. And as you position yourself in the places He desires to find you, it yields passport access and the release of a greater measure of His presence and power.

CHAPTER 5: Prayer

And the smoke of the incense, which came with
the prayers of the saints, ascended up before God
out of the angel's hand.
Revelations 8:4

Prayer is a conscious decision to communicate with God, which helps you develop an intimate spirit-to-spirit relationship with Him. Prayerful communion with God is by inspiration of the Holy Spirit. Communion and union with Him is the outcome of your focused attention to honor, worship and discover who He is to get an understanding of His virtues.

Getting God's attention through prayer invites Him to intervene in the affairs of the earth and your life. If you position yourself to learn about Him, to know His heart and mind, you will increasingly become aware of the open heaven access that brings the unseen into the seen— bringing kingdom blessings into manifestation. Prayer facilitates the manifestation of God's will and purpose.

1 Thesssalonians 5:17 says that we are to pray without ceasing. You can pray at anytime and in anyplace but find an ideal location where you are least likely to be interrupted or distracted. Many times when you make up your mind to pray, it seems that the phone will ring, someone will knock at the door, an urgent matter that needs your full attention will pop up, or you get sleepy. But prayer is the lifeblood to your spiritual health and wealth and often it will be necessary to press through hindrances. Do not relegate prayer to religious formality but allow it to be an opportunity to approach the presence of God with sincerity, humility of heart, and passion. You can offer up earnest, specific and bold prayers. Your bold access is accommodated by the imputed righteousness of Jesus Christ. *Seeing then that we have a great high priest, that is passed into the heavens, Jesus the Son of God, let us hold fast our profession. For we have not an high priest which cannot be touched with the feeling of our infirmities; but was in all points tempted like as we are, yet without sin. Let us therefore come boldly unto the throne of grace, that we may obtain mercy, and find grace to help in time of need.* Hebrews 4:14-16.

Prayer is your opportunity to ask forgiveness and deliverance from sin, iniquity and transgressions. God wants you to seek Him for the spiritual ability to crucify your flesh and to seek Him to obtain His will, agenda and council for your life. Prayer is two-way communication where you learn how to talk to God about your life experiences, relationships and circumstances, and in turn, learn to hear and know His voice. *So shall the knowledge of wisdom be unto thy soul: when thou hast found it, then there shall be a reward, and thy expectation shall not be cut off.* Proverbs 24:14

Prayer delivers the necessary spiritual sustenance to understand what is being ushered into the time and seasons of your life. *Call unto me, and I will answer thee, and shew thee great and mighty things, which thou knowest not.* Jeremiah 33:3

Through prayer you learn to know the MIND of God (His motives/methods, intentions, nourishment and details):

*M–Motives /Methods of God: You learn of His sovereignty, love, compassion, faithfulness, grace and mercy--*The counsel of the LORD standeth for ever, the thoughts of his heart to all generations.* Psalm 33:11

*I–Intentions toward you, His creation--*For I know the thoughts that I think toward you, saith the LORD, thoughts of peace, and not of evil, to give you an expected end.* Jeremiah 29:11

*N–Nourishment and provision—*But my God shall supply all your need according to his riches in glory by Christ Jesus.* Philippians 4:19

*D–Details of His will for your life--*And we know that all things work together for good to them that love God, to them who are the called according to his purpose.* Romans 8:28

You have the opportunity to know the HEART of God. The HEART of God is His character and the nature of His virtues. Some include holiness, expressions, authority, righteousness and truth:

*H–Holiness--*And ye shall be holy unto me: for I the LORD am holy, and have severed you from other people, that ye should be mine.* Leviticus 20:26

*E–Expressions--*O the depth of the riches both of the wisdom and knowledge of God! how unsearchable are his judgments, and his ways past finding out!* Romans 11:33

*A–Authority--*And they were all amazed, insomuch that they* *questioned among themselves, saying, What thing is this? what new doctrine is this? for with authority commandeth he even the unclean spirits, and they do obey him.* Mark 1:27

*R–Righteousness--*For the righteous LORD loveth righteousness; his countenance doth behold the upright.* Psalm 11:7

*T–Truth--*He is the Rock, his work is perfect: for all his ways are judgment: a God of truth and without iniquity, just and right is he.* Deuteronomy 32:4

Through prayer you can learn and know God's will for your assignment, purpose and destiny. Prayer also builds your faith in the scriptures and the covenant promises found in them. Faith is the assurance that you have been reconciled to God through the redemptive work of Jesus Christ. The confidence and faith in your salvation is that you are saved, healed, delivered, protected and possess the promise of eternal life with Him. Through faith you can have access to God in prayer. Through faith you gain the habitation or indwelling presence of the Holy Spirit (your comforter, helper and teacher) to become a fellow citizen of the household of God to believe that all things are possible.

The law of faith is to believe that He is. Faith says that He is a rewarder to those who seek Him diligently. If you begin to search, know, and believe what the scriptures say, then you will confess with your mouth to agree with God and His word. In addition, there is a progressive desire for the will of God to be accomplished in your life through knowledge and understanding of His scriptures.

Prayer establishes hope. When you HOPE in God, you will begin to:

*H–Hear Him through His word, prayer and your experiences-- *My sheep hear my voice, and I know them, and they follow me:* John 10:27

*O–Obey His word and submit to the care and charge of the pastor He has designated to shepherd over you--*And I will set up shepherds over them which shall feed them: and they shall fear no more, nor be dismayed, neither shall they be lacking, saith the LORD.* Jeremiah 23:4

*P–Pray the word of God without ceasing-- *Pray without ceasing.* 1Thessalonians 5:17

*E–Expect His response--*And it shall come to pass, that before they call, I will answer; and while they are yet speaking, I will hear.* Isaiah 65:24

When you HOPE in God, in return are some of His benefits.

*H–His Hearing ear--*But know that the LORD hath set apart him that is godly for himself: the LORD will hear when I call unto him.* Psalm 4:3

*O–Open heaven access to His presence--*Bring ye all the tithes into the storehouse, that there may be meat in mine house, and prove me now herewith, saith the LORD of hosts, if I will not open you the windows of heaven, and pour you out a blessing, that there shall not be room enough to receive it.* Malachi 3:10

*P–Peace while you wait for His response to your prayers--*The LORD will give strength unto his people; the LORD will bless his people with peace.* Psalm 29:11

*E–Eternal results--You have Christ in this world. You are not alien of the commonwealth of His kingdom. You are not a stranger to the covenant promises. You have His glory (the presence of His virtue) in your life. You have earnest, sincere expectations-- *Wherefore remember, that ye being in time past Gentiles in the flesh, who are called Uncircumcision by that which is called the Circumcision in the flesh made by hands; That at that time ye were without Christ, being aliens from the commonwealth of Israel, and strangers from the covenants of promise, having no hope, and without God in the world: But now in Christ Jesus ye who sometimes were far off are made nigh by the blood of Christ.* Ephesians 2:11-13

Prayer establishes TRUST in God.

*T–Turn to Him and tarry in His presence--*For the vision is yet for an appointed time, but at the end it shall speak, and not lie: though it tarry, wait for it; because it will surely come, it will not tarry.* Habakkuk 2:3

*R–Rest in and rely on His finished work—*But now the LORD my God hath given me rest on every side, so that there is neither adversary nor evil occurrent.* 1 Kings 5:4

*U–Understand His ways are not our ways--*For my thoughts are not your thoughts, neither are your ways my ways, saith the LORD.* Isaiah 55:8

*S–Surrender to Him--*Submit yourselves therefore to God. Resist the devil, and he will flee from you.* James 4:7

*T–Take Him at His word—*And they rose early in the morning, and went forth into the wilderness of Tekoa: and as they went forth, Jehoshaphat stood and said, Hear me, O Judah, and ye inhabitants of*

Jerusalem; Believe in the LORD your God, so shall ye be established; believe his prophets, so shall ye prosper. 2 Chronicles 20:20

Prayer will build you up and establish you in the faith. You are able to abound through and in His power. You can exercise spiritual authority, influence and dominion over natural and spiritual matters and circumstances. Prayer enables you to develop a relationship with God for an abiding life with His abiding presence. An abiding life in Jesus Christ will establish, cultivate, nourish and discipline your spirit, soul, mind and body.

Prayer reveals us in our fallen state, because our old identity prefers to be independent of God. The old nature believes that our own conscious is good or god. It has the attributes, characteristics, and disposition of and to sin. Personalities, traits, attitudes, behavior, and conduct defers to the flesh. But sin is a point of access and positions us for satan to attack, influence and dominate our lives.

Yielding and submitting to prayer aligns you to God's process of conforming you to His image. His processing is achieved by the divine activity of the Holy Spirit. Your "old man" nature and disposition is put to death through your proactive drawing on and working out of the indwelling presence and power of the Holy Spirit.

Processing by the Holy Spirit develops you for your new identity. This new identity prepares you for purpose and the fulfillment of your existence. During the process you will find that you're unable to fit everywhere and with everyone because God is developing you for a holy lifestyle and for service. Matthew 10:8 says that your reasonable service as a believer is to *Heal the sick, cleanse the lepers, raise the dead, cast out devils: freely ye have received, freely give.*

The Holy Spirit processes you to be clothed, covered and crowned for citizenship in the kingdom of God. He processes you for purification. Purification or consecration is giving up self, taking up your cross so that you desire a changed disposition. Prayer helps facilitate a renewed disposition that is dependent and reliant on God. The renewed man has a faithful and obedient nature toward God. A renewed nature will outwardly manifest the inner workings of the Holy Spirit.

God also processes you for sanctification. Our sanctification came through the finished work of Jesus Christ, the shedding of His blood to redeem us from the curse of the law, adjusting and aligning our carnal nature to a spiritual nature that is in right standing with God. *But we are bound to give thanks alway to God for you, brethren beloved of the Lord, because God hath from the beginning chosen you to salvation through sanctification of the Spirit and belief of the truth:* 1 Thessalonians 2:13.

Sanctification enables you to crucify your flesh, allowing the word of God to operate efficiently and effectively in and through your life. Through prayer, there is a perpetual transformation to His likeness. A Christ-like character confirms that the functional identity of Jesus Christ dwells in you. The results of sanctification, is an attachment and attentiveness of your senses to the things of God. Your flesh will not be easily subject to earthly influence or distractions, but rather, it becomes your nature to be circumspect in your thinking, your words and behavior. Through sanctification you are not subject or bound to man's opinions, philosophies or ideologies that excludes God (intellectualism). In addition, you will have lesser dependence on your abilities that do not glorify God (the arm of flesh).

The outcome of prayer brings about a transformation where 2 Corinthians 3:2 says, *Ye are our epistle written in our hearts, known and read of all men.* Prayer imparts an eternal and precious deposit to equip you and empower your gifts, talents and abilities. This impartation brings favor into your life and vindication from the residue of any shameful past. Your physical, mental or emotional persona won't reflect the wounds or scars left from experiences that satan may have used to try to destroy you.

Prayer gives you a greater desire and ability to disengage from the sources of corruptible influences or environments. It also develops, nurtures and strengthens a consciousness of God and His Kingdom. You gain a quicker and easier yieldedness to His will. Motives borne out of a right relationship with Jesus Christ is a life that desires to be pleasing in His sight. It is a life that desires to be taught how to become a spiritual partaker of His divine nature.

A spiritual partaker is a born-again child of God, filled with the Holy Spirit, progressively moving into sonship and heirship with Jesus Christ and God through obedience. *Whereby are given unto us exceeding great and precious promises: that by these ye might be partakers of the divine nature, having escaped the corruption that is in the world through lust.* 2 Peter 1:4.

The redemptive work of Jesus Christ has put you in right standing with God. His righteousness restored the original intent of God to you, and that was dominion. The authority you now possess is in the name of Jesus. His name activates power in heaven to give you dominion rights to decree, declare and proclaim the will of God in the heavens and the earth. The kingdom of God (the Holy Spirit) is in us to bear the righteous fruit of the Holy Spirit. You can bear the fruit of the spirit as long as there is a constant and obedient yieldedness and submission to what God orchestrates in your life, where He directs your steps, and how He sustains you. In other words, when God's agenda becomes your agenda through prayer and the divine assistance of the Holy Spirit, you can become a sure house of righteousness, joy and peace. *But the fruit of the Spirit is love, joy, peace, longsuffering, gentleness, goodness, faith, Meekness, temperance: against such there is no law.* Galatians 5:22-23. *For the fruit of the Spirit is in all goodness and righteousness and truth;* Ephesians 5:9.

As a spiritual partaker of the divine nature of Jesus Christ you are able to hear, see, receive, say and do what the word says. By hearing and heeding the word of God you should be in expectancy of divine results. When you see or observe the workings of the Holy Spirit in your life, you are discerning what God is doing or will do.

Receive the word of God gladly to embrace truth, life and peace. Be a spiritual partaker who speaks out the scriptures and decrees, declares and proclaims what God says. If you do what the word says to do, you are walking out or laboring in righteousness.

Signs, wonders and miracles will follow your life enabled with the power and divine resources of God. Manifestations of the gifts of the spirit will operate as kingdom authority enables you to have favorable effects on environmental elements and time. You can have the character and power to represent the kingdom of God through your words and actions, aligning yourself to spiritual order and protocol. There is open heaven access for you to become a steward of the mysteries of God where the potential of revelation can be limitless in levels, degrees, measures, realms and dimensions. *And he said, Unto you it is given to know the mysteries of the kingdom of God: but to others in parables; that seeing they might not see, and hearing they might not understand.* Luke 8:10.

Through a consistent and passionate prayer life you can discover the virtue of God. His virtue is revealed through His names. In the Book of Luke 2:36-38, we are told about a woman named Anna, a prophetess who did not depart from the temple. v36 *And there was one Anna, a prophetess, the daughter of Phanuel, of the tribe of Aser: she was of a great age, and had lived with an husband seven years from her virginity;*

v37 *And she was a widow of about fourscore and four years, which departed not from the temple, but served God with fastings and prayers night and day.*

v38 *And she coming in that instant gave thanks likewise unto the Lord, and spake of him to all them that looked for redemption in Jerusalem.*

Anna's consistent, passionate and fruitful prayer life no doubt caused her to learn and know the virtue (names) of God. Your dedication to prayer can ignite a passion to get into His presence, please Him through service and giving, and purify yourself. Passion provokes you to put God first, putting away idols or compromise that can steal your fire and devotion for Him. Your passion and desire should be to consecrate yourself to access a higher spiritual plain where you can become a God chaser and God pleaser.

Passion is zeal, excitement, strong feelings, eagerness, abandon, desire, hunger, thirst, love, strong affection, partiality, keen interest, preoccupation, worship, adoration, involvement, and thirst for knowledge. God becomes the object of your passion, devotion and affection. He is your beloved, heart's desire and your hope.

A passionless relationship with God is cold, unemotional, unloving, unaffectionate, uninterested. You are spiritually distant, insensitive, uninviting, unimaginative, spiritless, self-possessed, detached, uncommitted, and uninvolved.

In Luke's account of the life of Christ he commits three verses of scripture to tell us about Anna. He indicates that she was of a great age. In today's terms she would be considered a senior citizen. Her lineage was of the tribe of Asher. Asher's mother was Zilpah. When Laban gave Leah to Jacob he chose Zilpah as Leah's first handmaid. So Anna was considered one of God's chosen people.

Luke adds that she had been married. The bonds of marriage represents a natural as well as spiritual covenant. A covenant is a legal promise, contract, pact, treaty, bond, guarantee, or alliance. Anna's husband was her covering, companion, provision and protection. She must have felt secure in her husband's ability to protect and bring home the fruits of his labor. But after seven years, the scriptures say she was widowed. Anna is faced with a predicament. Her beloved husband, the object of her devotion, her provision, protection, companionship, and her passion is deceased.

She is now a victim of a broken marriage covenant through death. She has to present herself to what is considered the social services system of Jerusalem. Anna is positioned within the indigent class of people –the widows, orphans and the poor. She becomes a recipient of the benefit package God's law decreed for widows. In the wilderness God gave instruction to the children of Israel that the widow had His special protection. The Mosaic law decreed that they were not to be oppressed, or vexed. *Ye shall not afflict any widow, or fatherless child.* Exodus 22:22. If so they could plead their case before a judge. Creditors could not take or levy their raiment (clothing). *Thou shalt not pervert the judgment of the stranger, nor of the fatherless; nor take a widow's raiment to pledge:* Deuteronomy 24:17

For provision or to support themselves, widows were allowed to come behind the reapers and glean in the fields and vineyards. *When thou cuttest down thine harvest in thy field, and hast forgot a sheaf in the field, thou shalt not go again to fetch it: it shall be for the stranger, for the fatherless, and for the widow: that the LORD thy God may bless thee in all the work of thine hands. When thou beatest thine olive tree, thou shalt not go over the boughs again: it shall be for the stranger, for the fatherless, and for the widow. When thou gatherest the grapes of thy vineyard, thou shalt not glean it afterward: it shall be for the stranger, for the fatherless, and for the widow.* Deuteronomy 24:19-21.

Anna was married for only seven years and Luke does not indicate that she had any children. If she did, they wouldn't have been old enough to work or help support her. Anna had to depend on the law of God to have a lifestyle quite possibly materially beneath what she had been accustomed to while she was married. Her very existence was bound to the consequences of a broken marriage covenant.

You don't have to be a widow to endure the consequences of broken promises and broken covenants. For instance, you can be someone who has a perfect job, enjoying and getting paid well for what you do. But one day your employer might call you into the office to inform you of job cuts. Rent and all the bills you won't be able to pay will stress you out. It's because of broken covenants. Your broken covenant with the job will cause broken covenants with your landlord and creditors.

Or you can be someone who thinks you're all right with God. Money is no object, but you are unhappily married, you don't spend time with your children, and feel emptiness or voids in your life. You might attend church regularly. In fact, you've been going all your life, but you rarely praise and worship the Lord. You're tired, bored, burned out and it's hard to focus. You can't pay attention in church during the pastor's message. You don't make time to read or study the scriptures or pray. And when you do, it's in bed, but you fall asleep almost before you begin.

In each case, you have broken covenants of another kind. Broken covenant with your marriage, to your children, to your emotional, physical and spiritual health and well being. Do you have broken covenants with family, career, responsibilities or God? Then it's time to find and "depart not from the temple" through the scriptures and prayer.

We don't know how long Anna lived in a lifestyle as a widow. But one day she came into the temple to honor God, maybe even to pay a vow. We are not told what determined her decision to remain in the temple. A divine appointment for a divine encounter with her God was the point in Anna's life, where Luke says, "she departed not from the temple." She chose to seek and pursue God in His temple.

Since Acts 2, we the believer are the temple of the Holy Spirit. How can we, like Anna, "depart not from the temple?" It is by making a voluntary decision to seek and pursue God with our Helper the Holy Spirit. Anna made a decision to enter into a new covenant, an eternal covenant with God. She decided to put herself on God's agenda, choosing to step into kingdom territory (the temple), refusing to come out. Out of that decision the Word says, she served Him through a devotion to fasting, prayers, night and day.

When Anna made a conscious and resolute decision to enter into an eternal covenant with God, to ignite her passion for Him, she aligned herself to experience the virtues of God through His presence. Of course she may have been restricted to designated places in the temple because she was not a priest. Wherever she was allowed to be, she committed herself to never departing from it because she must have discovered that in His presence there are dwelling places.

When you enter into God's presence through prayer, you are establishing an eternal covenant with Him. You can enter into a dwelling place where you find His virtue, the Lord your provider. In addition to your natural needs, He will provide you with spiritual food. Your daily bread, *And Jesus answered him, saying, It is written, That man shall not live by bread alone, but by every word of God.* Luke 4:4. He will provide His sincere milk, *As newborn babes, desire the sincere milk of the word, that ye may grow thereby:* 1 Peter 2:2. And He will provide the strong meat, *But strong meat belongeth to them that are of full age, even those who by reason of use have their senses exercised to discern both good and evil.* Hebrews 5:14. Your eternal, necessary food is all in the form of the Word and for your spiritual age (level of spiritual maturity).

He daily loads you down with benefits. *Blessed be the Lord, who daily loadeth us with benefits, even the God of our salvation. Selah.* Psalm 68:19. He gives the oil, which is the anointing you need to serve Him with joy and gladness. *Thou lovest righteousness, and hatest wickedness: therefore God, thy God, hath anointed thee with the oil of gladness above thy fellows.* Psalm 45:7.

In this dwelling place of His presence, you find wisdom, knowledge and understanding of the Word of God, His anointing and joy. It is a place of processing and preparation that comes from prayer, hearing, reading and learning and most importantly speaking out the scriptures. You need the anointing that comes from the transformation and renewal that the Word and a prayer life brings. When we pray, we can get into God's presence where He reveals His virtue, Jehovah-Jireh, the Lord will provide. *And Abraham said, My son, God will provide himself a lamb for a burnt offering: so they went both of them together.* Genesis 22:8.

When you ignite your passion for God through prayer, you will find the dwelling place of communion, a place of prayer and meditation with the scriptures. As you read and speak out the scriptures, you are savoring them for your spiritual growth and development. The Word of God is the bread of life, the milk, the strong meat and the joy of the Lord, which gives you strength. You will bear an anointing that is the physical evidence or witness of what God and His Word is doing in your life.

At times this place of His presence will demand fasting and/or partaking of a diet of scripture God customizes for your circumstance. When I want to know more about God, as I pray, I focus on scriptures that reveal His mighty acts, or His mind and heart. There were times of illness and infirmities where I focused on healing scriptures and found great peace and comfort in them. I have found hope when I was unsettled about situations and circumstance in my life. God ministered the words and power of deliverance when I was bound by depression and oppression. He is a spiritual dietician who imparts health and strength to your spirit and satisfies your soul. In the dwelling place of His presence, God reveals himself as Jehovah-Rohi, the Lord my shepherd. *A Psalm of David. The LORD is my shepherd; I shall not want.* Psalm 23:1.

Another dwelling place of His presence is where you and God commune with one another. You offer up songs or prayers of thanksgiving, praise and worship. It is where you dedicate your mind, heart, soul and spirit to Him alone. *Sing unto him, sing Psalm unto him, talk ye of all his wondrous works.* 1 Chronicles 16:9.

In this place of God's presence, He has shown me who and what to fellowship with--who and what I can entertain. What is it about your life, associations or environment that He might be saying "No" or "Yes" to? Does who and what you fellowship with or entertain please God? Are you praying to find out? When you pray do you listen and obey?

He will not abandon or forsake your prayers and fellowship of thanksgiving, praise and worship. It will draw a greater measure of His presence, at times so tangible to the natural senses. *And he said, It is not the voice of them that shout for mastery, neither is it the voice of them that cry for being overcome: but the noise of them that sing do I hear.* Exodus 32:18. He is Jehovah-Shammah, the Lord is there. *It was round about eighteen thousand measures: and the name of the city from that day shall be, The LORD is there.* Ezekiel 48:35.

This dwelling place is also where you find life and peace during your fellowship with Him. Does your fellowship with God re-energize, refresh and renew your spirit and bring you peace? In this dwelling place His virtue is Jehovah-Elyon, the Lord most high. *I will praise the LORD according to his righteousness: and will sing praise to the name of the LORD most high.* Psalm 7:17.

When you "depart not from the temple" through prayer you will find a dwelling place of cleansing and purging. It is where you are spiritually cleaned up, cleaned out and stripped naked before God. This place has spiritual mirrors and God has strategically placed them so you won't see anyone else but you. Daily, God draws me to this place of His presence and causes my spiritual eyes to be opened to reveal me to me. I have the opportunity to see and acknowledge my natural and spiritual wretchedness when He wants to deal with what is on and in me.

No matter how perfect you think you are, spiritually naked before God, everything gets exposed. We all know that you can't bathe and get clean with your clothes on. You have to strip to get clean. In His presence He washes you with the water of His word. As you spend time to pray and study the word, you will realize that His presence exposes the things you missed or avoided when He told you to consecrate yourself. When I have acknowledged my sin or transgressions and submitted to the truth of the Word and the power of His presence, I have found over and over again, that He removes the spots, blemishes, and blots I couldn't reach or fix myself. I have received His deliverance from entanglements with people, places and issues that required His sovereign, merciful, gracious and powerful intervention.

God unctions you to consecrate your eyes for proper observations, and to clean out your ears to hear His voice. My pastor, Dr. Robbie Horton says, hear Him accurately, precisely and distinctly. *Who shall ascend into the hill of the LORD? or who shall stand in his holy place? He that hath clean hands, and a pure heart; who hath not lifted up his soul unto vanity, nor sworn deceitfully.* Psalm 24:3-4. *Draw nigh to God, and he will draw nigh to you. Cleanse your hands, ye sinners; and purify your hearts, ye double minded.* James 4:8.

In this place of His presence you learn to discern your times and seasons. What are you consuming and allowing to digest into your temple that could defile it? Every day, I make a decision to consecrate my mouth to change my speech so I might have a word in due season for the weary and the law of kindness on my lips. *Deliver my soul, O LORD, from lying lips, and from a deceitful tongue.* Psalm 120:2. *For he that will love life, and see good days, let him refrain his tongue from evil, and his lips that they speak no guile:* 1 Peter 3:10.

In the natural, impurities inside you have to come out. This is even so in the spirit. Everything that is not like God, that bloats or puffs you up, like anger, lying, vanity and pride, everything that is not pleasing to Him has to be purged. Trying to hold on to a temperament that defiles your temple will eventually cause spiritual death. You have to go to the bathroom everyday, several times a day. You can't avoid it if you want to get healthy and stay healthy naturally and spiritually. In this dwelling place during prayer, you submit your whole body, mind, soul and spirit to consecration for holiness. *Having therefore these promises, dearly beloved, let us cleanse ourselves from all filthiness of the flesh and spirit, perfecting holiness in the fear of God.* 2 Corinthians 7:1. *If we confess our sins, he is faithful and just to forgive us our sins, and to cleanse us from all unrighteousness.* 1 John 1:9. When we consecrate ourselves and submit to the sanctifying power of God, He reveals Himself as Jehovah-Mekaddishkem, the Lord our sanctifier. *And ye shall keep my statutes, and do them: I am the LORD which sanctify you.* Leviticus 20:8

God's presence brings natural and spiritual healing and deliverance. There is a balm in Gilead and the oil of joy that is better than a band-aid, better than antiseptic, better than ointments, and better than pills. When we pursue God through prayer we can access His dwelling place where He reveals Himself as Jehovah-Rapha, the Lord my Healer. *...I will put none of these diseases upon thee, which I have brought upon the Egyptians: for I am the LORD that healeth thee.* Exodus 15:26.

God has a dwelling place where His presence is a spiritual covering for your head, your body, and feet. God inspects your spiritual wardrobe daily. Just as we concern ourselves with natural garments, we should also keep the spiritual garments open for inspection. Are they clean, are they torn, are they in order, do they fit properly, and most of all are they yours? Do you have the proper garment for the proper occasion? *Thou hast a few names even in Sardis which have not defiled their garments; and they shall walk with me in white: for they are worthy.* Revelations 3:4. *Behold, I come as a thief. Blessed is he that watcheth, and keepeth his garments, lest he walk naked, and they see his shame.* Revelations 16:15.

When you allow God to have His perfecting work in you, He transforms, prepares, builds and establishes your spiritual wardrobe. It will be the proper wardrobe for your age, the time and season of your life, for your purpose, and your future. He will perfect your garments daily. Your natural garments will reflect what He has done in you spiritually. He will dress you with Himself—the spiritual garments that only He can form, fashion and clothe you with—even a robe of righteousness. *I will greatly rejoice in the LORD, my soul shall be joyful in my God; for he hath clothed me with the garments of salvation, he hath covered me with the robe of righteousness, as a bridegroom decketh himself with ornaments, and as a bride adorneth herself with her jewels.* Isaiah 61:10. God is Jehovah-Tsidkenu, the Lord our righteousness. *In his days Judah shall be saved, and Israel shall dwell safely: and this is his name whereby he shall be called, THE LORD OUR RIGHTEOUSNESS.* Jeremiah 23:6.

Just as you have a natural closet, you have a spiritual closet with God. This closet is your meeting place into His presence for all manner of prayer. Your armor for prayer and warfare, for supplication, thanksgiving, praise, worship and intercession is found here. *For we wrestle not against flesh and blood, but against principalities, against powers, against the rulers of the darkness of this world, against spiritual wickedness in high places. Wherefore take unto you the whole armour of God, that ye may be able to withstand in the evil day, and having done all, to stand. Stand therefore, having your loins girt about with truth, and having on the breastplate of righteousness; And your feet shod with the preparation of the gospel of peace; Above all, taking the shield of faith, wherewith ye shall be able to quench all the fiery darts of the wicked. And take the helmet of salvation, and the sword of the Spirit, which is the word of God: Praying always with all prayer and supplication in the Spirit, and watching thereunto with all perseverance and supplication for all saints;* Ephesians 6:12-18.

In this dwelling place, the Lord is Jehovah-Sabaoth, the Lord of host. *And this man went up out of his city yearly to worship and to sacrifice unto the LORD of hosts in Shiloh...* 1 Samuel 1:3.

Luke says Anna prayed day and night in the natural. Spiritually, she prayed in the day–the seasons of good times and blessings. She prayed in the night—the seasons of challenge, darkness, valleys, the desert places and the wilderness. She prayed at all times without ceasing. In this dwelling place of His presence, you learn how to pray in the day and night seasons of your life. Most people tend to pray only during the "night" for emergencies, crisis or urgent needs. I believe it is more important to pray when times are good, during the "day seasons." He is not a "gimme" God that you go after only when you need to satisfy your earthbound needs. When you pray in the "day" it reveals your desire to seek and know God's face, mind and heart. You will discover His protective presence and the virtue of Jehovah-Nissi, the Lord my banner. *And Moses built an altar, and called the name of it Jehovahnissi:* Exodus 17:15.

God has a dwelling place where His presence is a place of rest, of ceasing from your own labor. It is a place of security and trust. As you rest in God, even sleep, you submit yourself in trusting abandon to the safety and protection of God. *I will both lay me down in peace, and sleep: for thou, LORD, only makest me dwell in safety.* Psalm 4:8. This dwelling place is where He becomes your refuge and it is a place of intimacy. *Be still, and know that I am God: I will be exalted among the heathen, I will be exalted in the earth.* Psalm 46:10. You allow God to minister His love and peace back to you. He reminds you of who you are and whose you are. The Lord reveals His mind--so you can have the mind of Christ. He reveals His heart to you--where you learn and know the heartbeat of God.

God reveals Himself to you as you rest and yield to His presence. He is Jehovah-Shalom, the Lord of our peace. *Then Gideon built an altar there unto the LORD, and called it Jehovah-shalom: unto this day it is yet in Ophrah of the Abiezrites.* Judges 6:24.

In His presence the Lord imparts what He can entrust to you. You conceive destiny and purpose, then you will have to go back to the closet to travail and birth it out. *That the God of our Lord Jesus Christ, the Father of glory, may give unto you the spirit of wisdom and revelation in the knowledge of him: The eyes of your understanding being enlightened; that ye may know what is the hope of his calling, and what the riches of the glory of his inheritance in the saints, And what is the exceeding greatness of his power to us-ward who believe, according to the working of his mighty power,* Ephesians 1:17-19.

When you ignite your passion for God through prayer it is possible to visit the aforementioned dwelling places everyday. He gives 24 hours /7 days-a-week invitations and the enabling ability through the Holy Spirit to meet and fellowship with Him. He will provoke you to seek out, and become familiar with every facet of His presence. Do you want to be so fascinated with God that you will inquire of Him like Moses? *And he said, I beseech thee, shew me thy glory.* Exodus 33:18.

The Prophetess Anna was 84 years old. She lived a long devoted life to God serving Him with prayer and fasting, day and night. She must have become familiar with some of His dwelling places. The day she decided to "depart not from the temple" transformed her life. Her steps were ordered of the Lord. She was in step and in the perfect timing of the Lord such that when she entered into a certain part of the temple, Luke says, "in that instant," perfect timing caused her to witness Simeon speaking blessing over the young child Jesus Christ. And Luke says "Anna gave thanks likewise unto the Lord." She came into agreement with a "Yes" and "Amen" to Simeon's blessing of Jesus.

Because of her devotion to the temple and because she tapped into God's presence with her prayers and fasting, Anna was able to serve God for years without burning out. She served Him with joy and gladness. I know the Lord was pleased with Anna. He is a rewarder to those who diligently seek Him and He gives back and renews your strength.

Anna sowed her life to God in the temple, therefore she was witness to the manifestation of a promise made to Simeon. The promise was that he would not see death until his eyes beheld the Lord's Christ (the anointed one). *And it was revealed unto him by the Holy Ghost, that he should not see death, before he had seen the Lord's Christ.* Luke 2:26. When Anna blessed the Lord likewise to rejoice over Simeon's blessing, she received an unexpected blessing herself. *And she coming in that instant gave thanks likewise unto the Lord,and spake of him to all them that looked for redemption in Jerusalem.* Luke 2:38.

Do you rejoice with those who rejoice? Anna had another divine encounter with God where she was able to see the face of Jesus, the Messiah, the Saviour and Redeemer of all men. When Anna decided to depart not from the temple, she positioned herself to be processed for a divine appointment to receive a divine encounter. Her eyes beheld the manifested Son of God. She had the opportunity to touch the Anointed One. Anna's experiences were orchestrated by God. She wasn't too old to be released into a prophetic ministry beyond the walls of the temple.

49

How long have you been waiting for your release to serve God in a ministerial capacity? Luke says Anna was a prophetess because she spake of Him (Jesus) to all who looked for redemption. God put a witness and testimony in Anna's mouth so that all who believed, trusted and hoped in the promise of the Messiah, would know that He had come. The widow Anna was a prophetess AND evangelist.

At a young age, Anna made a decision to "depart not from the temple." Whatever was the basis for her decision, she received the manifestation of a promise given in Isaiah 54:1 which says: *Sing, O barren, thou that didst not bear* (that was Anna); *break forth into singing* (in the dwelling place of Jehovah-Elyon, the Lord most high), *and cry aloud* (in the dwelling place of Jehovah-Sabaoth, the Lord of host), *thou that didst not travail with child: for more are the children of the desolate than the children of the married wife, saith the LORD.* Anna was a childless widow who birthed out spiritual children into the kingdom of God through her dedication to prayer, fasting and her testimony of the Messiah's coming.

She made a decision in her state of desolation as a widow, a place of broken covenant, to enter and not depart from the temple. She preferred God over any and everything. She made herself separate and available to the Lord, with dedication to a lifestyle of humility and daily sacrifice. She created an environment and dwelling place in her heart for God. She gave Him access to her heart (affections), her mind (thoughts), her soul (will and choices) and her might (resources).

Anna consecrated herself for holiness and God consciousness: loving what He loves, hating what He hates. And because she gave Him access to her dwelling places by drawing nigh to Him, God drew nigh, giving her access to His dwelling places. Ultimately, she revealed outwardly what was inwardly developed. Anna is an example to us, that no matter what station in life we are in—the high or low places-- no matter what age, or gender, we are to ignite our passion for God through prayer. It is through prayer that we can access all the dwelling places of His presence. *Blessed is the man whom thou choosest, and causest to approach unto thee, that he may dwell in thy courts: we shall be satisfied with the goodness of thy house, even of thy holy temple.* Psalm 65:4.

Today, your life does not have to be one of desolation, confusion or sickness. You don't have to be passionless. Even if everything seems perfect in your life, you still need to ignite your passion for God through prayer. Prayer is praise, thanksgiving, supplication, worship, intercession, and meditation. To enter into the presence of God in any of these levels require that we remember and acknowledge that God is holy and we must come before Him in holiness.

To approach Him in holiness is to come with a repentant heart, mind, soul and spirit. Approach Him as Jehovah-Mekaddishkem, the Lord our sanctifier, repentant of anything that would hinder answered prayer. Hinderances include sin, iniquity, transgressions, idolatry, incorrect motives, fear, condemnation, doubt, unbelief, unforgiveness, bitterness, the cares of the world, lack of faith or not knowing the Word of God. You can appropriate the redemptive work, righteousness and the name of Jesus Christ as your authority to enter into His presence.

Approach God with thanksgiving, praise and worship by declaring, proclaiming and decreeing the word over your supplications and petitions. When you declare Him Jehovah-Shammah, the Lord who is there, you can affirm your belief and faith in God, keeping your heart in expectancy that He will answer your request or fulfill your desires.

The scriptures say to enter His gates with thanksgiving. Approach God with thanksgiving to reverence His Power, edifying His strength and might, His rule, sovereignty, distinction and lordship. He is Jehovah-Elyon, the Lord most high. Thanksgiving helps you develop humility as you keep your focus on God and His kingdom.

Enter His courts with praise to esteem Him greatly, reverencing His name and authority. Praising God demonstrates your pleasure in knowing of Him, your joyfulness over belonging to Him, blessing His name, showing deference to Him, your adoration, reverence, and celebrating His virtues.

The tabernacle in the wilderness had an outer and inner court. The outer court was where the altar of sacrifice was located. The inner court in the tabernacle was the place of the oil, lampstand and incense. Now, we are the living tabernacle of the Holy Spirit. So when you enter the outer courts through prayer and praise, it is the place where you repent and surrender everything to God. The inner court is where you make your supplication and petitions known. It is a place of sacrifice, intercession, warfare and worship. Supplication and petitions are presenting your cares or needs. As you interact with God in supplication it is to seek His provisions of supply, health, well-being, direction and assistance.

Worship God to acknowledge who He is toward you and to acknowledge His character. Communion and fellowship through worship develops your spiritual ears to be open to hear and listen to Him and the opportunity to wait in His presence. Approaching God in worship is to exalt Him with accolades, recognition and magnification of His virtues. Also crown Him, proclaim His loftiness, fame, favor. To worship God is to boast of His omniscience (He is all knowing), His omnipotence (He is all power) and His omnipresence (He is all and in all).

Worshiping the Lord in spirit and in truth will lead you into the Holy of Holies. Through prayer we can reach the place of His presence known as the secret place or the dwelling place of God's glory and holiness. It is a place of reverence, of awe and stillness, a quiet place where He is Jehovah-Shalom. The scriptures say that no flesh shall glory in His presence. When you access the Holy of Holies you are where His presence and majesty enables you to experience peace, intimacy, communion and fellowship. Positionally you are at God's feet, waiting to hear His voice as you soak in His presence.

INTERCESSORY PRAYER

And I sought for a man among them, that should make up the hedge, and stand in the gap before me for the land, that I should not destroy it: but I found none. Ezekiel 22:30
And he saw that there was no man, and wondered that there was no intercessor: therefore his arm brought salvation unto him; and his righteousness, it sustained him. Isaiah 59:16

The byproduct of a committed prayer life is the ability and wisdom to warfare and travail in the spirit through intercession, to bring forth or birth out what is revealed in the spirit into the natural realm. Intercession is warfare, standing in the gap on behalf of other people, situations and circumstances.

Intercessory prayers uncover, cancel, nullify, bind, uproot and tear down satan's access, assignments and effects. Intercession can render satan and his obstacles powerless and in it's place release, build and plant kingdom alternatives.

When you approach God with intercession you acknowledge His authority and dominion. Prayers of intercession affect the world, kingdoms, systems, institutions, communities, families and individuals. It avails you the opportunity to exercise faith in your dominion and authority to speak in God's behalf.

An intercessor is a spiritual watchman or one who keeps an offensive and defensive posture in the spirit. The intercessor looks out for spiritual messages or instructions for when to open or close spiritual access. They keep an awareness of the spiritual activity of the enemy; and are able to foresee through revelation, which may result in a prophecy, word of wisdom or a word of knowledge going forth.

As a doorkeeper / gatekeeper they discern what to allow into the earth realm, to open and close spiritual doors, gates, access points, portals, and invite the work of the Holy Spirit. The intercessor binds the plans, assignments and work of principalities, powers and evil forces and makes reassignments to the alternatives and will of God.

Intercessory prayers counteract ruin or destruction by proclaiming and decreeing the Word of God to plant kingdom solutions. A spiritually alert and attentive intercessor will be able to perceive and observe what others fail to see. They build defensive spiritual hedges, walls and boundaries. It is important to vigilantly maintain spiritual vision, health, integrity and anointing.

Intercession is mandated for world leaders, systems, and issues that oppose God. Issues that oppose God are sin, iniquity, transgression, idolatry and all forms of wickedness. Those who don't know God, the harvest of souls, needs of family, friends and others, and most importantly every facet of the church is laid upon God's heart for our intercession.

As believers, we have been given the ministry of reconciliation. And all things are of God, who hath reconciled us to himself by Jesus Christ, and hath given to us the ministry of reconciliation; 2 Corinthians 5:18. That means that everyone, not just a handful of designated people can and should intercede. There is a responsibility to pray not only for ourselves but for others. We are to intercede for truth, justice, and righteousness to prevail by praying scriptural affirmations, proclamations, declarations, and decrees.

MEDITATION

Finally, brethren, whatsoever things are true, whatsoever things are honest, whatsoever things are just, whatsoever things are pure, whatsoever things are lovely, whatsoever things are of good report; if there be any virtue, and if there be any praise, think on these things.
Philippians 4:8

Another method of prayer is Meditation. Meditation is focused thought, reflection and contemplation of God's Word, His work, His nature and His abilities.

One definition of meditation is to utter, groan, or ponder. It also means to rehearse in one's mind, or contemplate. An example is discursive meditation, which is pondering the text of the scriptures. Another definition is to dwell diligently, consider and heed, as in affective prayer or contemplative meditation. Affective prayer is inquiring of God about scripture to seek the meaning, understanding and revelation of the truth. Contemplative meditation is resting in the presence of the Lord.

Prayer through thanksgiving, praise, worship, intercession or meditation is a phenomenal spirit-to-spirit opportunity. In the holy place of God's presence, you will begin to learn and experience some of the virtues of God. According to scripture and through the result of consistent communion you will find that God, *is exalted above all gods, He sits on the circle of the earth, He is the Lord our maker. He reigns over all creation. He is the wonderful counselor, everlasting father and the prince of peace. He is knowledge, wisdom, understanding and might, he is sovereign, the wheel in the middle of the wheel. He shall endure forever, He is God alone, a righteous judge, the Lord most high. He dwelleth in Zion, He is king forever, the highest, perfect in strength, governor among the nations, the King of glory, and Lord of hosts. He is upright, the God of truth, goodness, He is marvelous, He is mercy, faithful, longsuffering, lovingkindness, the fountain of life, peace, the Lord God of Israel, the living God, most high, Lord of lords, king over all the earth, mighty God, judge in the earth. He has all power, he is Jehovah, Adoni, Eloyhim, Yahweh God, the almighty, the Holy one of Israel. He has all dominion, power, authority, He is glorious, good, strong and mighty, mighty in battle, a sun and shield, full of compassion, patient, kind, the most high over all the earth. He is gracious, plentious in truth, omnipotent, omniscient, omnipresent, and upright. He is the creator of all things, great in Zion, slow to anger, very great, clothed with honor and majesty. He is the all sufficient one, a consuming fire, great and awesome, a light, there is none like him. He is greatly to be feared, He is holy, perfect, upright, and worthy to be praised.*

Through a relationship with God borne out of prayer, you will learn to know, experience and declare what He does for you. *He is the deliverer, our redeemer, a guide, teacher, preserver, our shield, our banner, father to the fatherless, a judge of the widows. He is our counselor, a portion forever, our refuge, rock, fortress, buckler, and horn of our salvation. He is a high tower, a hiding place, our helper and a present help in the day of trouble, our sure defense, a shelter, a strong tower, the rock of our strength, a strong habitation, a dwelling place. He corrects, reproves, instructs, chastens, and rebukes us. He is the comforter, He preserveth the soul, He is forgiving, a healer, satisfies us with good things, gracious, opens His hands and satisfies every living thing, the lifter of our head. He is the God of our salvation, the strength of our life, the health of our countenance, our guide, hope, and trust, not far from us, our abundance and increase. He will spare the poor, He speaks and we hear, He is the supplier of all our needs. He is love, joy, patience, happiness, He is our keeper, and His goodness follows us all the days of our life.*

Whatever methods you employ, through prayer and the knowledge of the scriptures, to facilitate access and audience with our creator you will reap the reward of experiencing a foretaste of His infinite glory. When you "Pray What God Says" then you will taste and see that the Lord is Good!

CHAPTER 6: Topical Scriptures
to
"Pray What God Says"

The following pages contain several topical scriptures relative to areas that concern our daily life. Knowledge of what these and other scriptures you search out for yourself, say about a particular topic will assist you in developing a unique, fruitful and foundationally sound prayer life. Isaiah 45:11 says *Thus saith the LORD, the Holy One of Israel, and his Maker, Ask me of things to come concerning my sons, and concerning the work of my hands command ye me.*

As you pray, allow the Holy Spirit to bring the scriptures to your remembrance so that your thanksgiving, praise, worship and times of soaking in the presence of the Lord will yield effectual, fervent prayers that availeth much. So "Pray What God Says."

SPIRITUAL GROWTH

Honoring the Glory of God
1 Chronicles 16:27 -- *Glory and honour are in his presence;*
strength and gladness are in his place.

1 Chronicles 16:28 -- Give unto the LORD, ye kindreds of the people, give unto the LORD glory and strength.

1 Peter 1:8 -- Whom having not seen, ye love; in whom, though now ye see him not, yet believing, ye rejoice with joy unspeakable and full of glory:

1 Thessalonians 2:12 -- That ye would walk worthy of God, who hath called you unto his kingdom and glory.

Deuteronomy 5:24 -- And ye said, Behold, the LORD our God hath shewed us his glory and his greatness, and we have heard his voice out of the midst of the fire: we have seen this day that God doth talk with man, and he liveth.

Psalm 24:7 -- Lift up your heads, O ye gates; and be ye lift up, ye everlasting doors; and the King of glory shall come in.

Psalm 104:31 -- The glory of the LORD shall endure forever: the LORD shall rejoice in his works.

Psalm 148:13 -- Let them praise the name of the LORD: for his name alone is excellent; his glory is above the earth and heaven.

Righteousness
Psalm 106:3 -- *Blessed are they that keep judgment,*
and he that doeth righteousness at all times.

1 Peter 3:14 -- But and if ye suffer for righteousness' sake, happy are ye: and be not afraid of their terror, neither be troubled;

1 Timothy 6:11 -- But thou, O man of God, flee these things; and follow after righteousness, godliness, faith, love, patience, meekness.

Colossians 3:3-4 -- For ye are dead, and your life is hid with Christ in God. When Christ, who is our life, shall appear, then shall ye also appear with him in glory.

Ephesians 5:9 -- For the fruit of the Spirit is in all goodness and righteousness and truth;

Ephesians 6:14 -- Stand therefore, having your loins girt about with truth, and having on the breastplate of righteousness;

Isaiah 54:14 -- In righteousness shalt thou be established: thou shalt be far from oppression; for thou shalt not fear: and from terror; for it shall not come near thee.

Matthew 5:6 -- Blessed are they which do hunger and thirst after righteousness: for they shall be filled.

Matthew 6:33 -- But seek ye first the kingdom of God, and his righteousness; and all these things shall be added unto you.

Philippians 3:9 -- And be found in him, not having mine own righteousness, which is of the law, but that which is through the faith of Christ, the righteousness which is of God by faith:

Psalm 1:1-2 -- Blessed is the man that walketh not in the counsel of the ungodly, nor standeth in the way of sinners, nor sitteth in the seat of the scornful. But his delight is in the law of the LORD; and in his law doth he meditate day and night.

Romans 12:1 -- I beseech you therefore, brethren, by the mercies of God, that ye present your bodies a living sacrifice, holy, acceptable unto God, which is your reasonable service.

Romans 14:19 -- Let us therefore follow after the things which make for peace, and things wherewith one may edify another.

Romans 14:17 -- For the kingdom of God is not meat and drink; but righteousness, and peace, and joy in the Holy Ghost.

Anointing / Presence of Holy Spirit

Psalm 92:10 -- But my horn shalt thou exalt like the horn of an unicorn: I shall be anointed with fresh oil.

1 John 2:27 -- But the anointing which ye have received of him abideth in you, and ye need not that any man teach you: but as the same anointing teacheth you of all things, and is truth, and is no lie, and even as it hath taught you, ye shall abide in him.

Isaiah 10:27 -- And it shall come to pass in that day, that his burden shall be taken away from off thy shoulder, and his yoke from off thy neck, and the yoke shall be destroyed because of the anointing.

Isaiah 61:1 -- The Spirit of the Lord GOD is upon me; because the LORD hath anointed me to preach good tidings unto the meek; he hath sent me to bind up the brokenhearted, to proclaim liberty to the captives, and the opening of the prison to them that are bound;

Psalm 23:5 -- Thou preparest a table before me in the presence of mine enemies: thou anointest my head with oil; my cup runneth over.

Psalm 45:7 -- Thou lovest righteousness, and hatest wickedness: therefore God, thy God, hath anointed thee with the oil of gladness above thy fellows.

Obedience to God's Will
Genesis 22:18 -- And in thy seed shall all the nations of the earth be blessed; because thou hast obeyed my voice.

John 15:7 -- If ye abide in me, and my words abide in you, ye shall ask what ye will, and it shall be done unto you.

1 John 1:10 -- If we say that we have not sinned, we make him a liar, and his word is not in us.

1 John 3:22 -- And whatsoever we ask, we receive of him, because we keep his commandments, and do those things that are pleasing in his sight.

1 John 5:3 -- For this is the love of God, that we keep his commandments: and his commandments are not grievous.

1 Timothy 4:12 -- Let no man despise thy youth; but be thou an example of the believers, in word, in conversation, in charity, in spirit, in faith, in purity.

2 Peter 3:18 -- But grow in grace, and in the knowledge of our Lord and Saviour Jesus Christ. To him be glory both now and for ever. Amen.

2 Timothy 4:2 -- Preach the word; be instant in season, out of season; reprove, rebuke, exhort with all longsuffering and doctrine.

Colossians 3:16 -- Let the word of Christ dwell in you richly in all wisdom; teaching and admonishing one another in Psalm and hymns and spiritual songs, singing with grace in your hearts to the Lord.

Deuteronomy 11:27 -- A blessing, if ye obey the commandments of the LORD your God, which I command you this day:

Deuteronomy 28:2 -- And all these blessings shall come on thee, and overtake thee, if thou shalt hearken unto the voice of the LORD thy God.

Ephesians 6:17 -- And take the helmet of salvation, and the sword of the Spirit, which is the word of God:

Hebrews 4:12 -- For the word of God is quick, and powerful, and sharper than any two-edged sword, piercing even to the dividing asunder of soul and spirit, and of the joints and marrow, and is a discerner of the thoughts and intents of the heart.

Isaiah 1:19 -- If ye be willing and obedient, ye shall eat the good of the land:

James 1:22 -- But be ye doers of the word, and not hearers only, deceiving your own selves.

John 14:15 -- If ye love me, keep my commandments.

John 14:23 -- Jesus answered and said unto him, If a man love me, he will keep my words: and my Father will love him, and we will come unto him, and make our abode with him.

John 15:14 -- Ye are my friends, if ye do whatsoever I command you.

Proverbs 30:5 -- Every word of God is pure: he is a shield unto them that put their trust in him.

Psalm 1:2 -- But his delight is in the law of the LORD; and in his law doth he meditate day and night.

Psalm 25:10 -- All the paths of the LORD are mercy and truth unto such as keep his covenant and his testimonies.

Psalm 111:10 -- The fear of the LORD is the beginning of wisdom: a good understanding have all they that do his commandments: his praise endureth for ever.

Psalm 119:11 -- Thy word have I hid in mine heart, that I might not sin against thee.

Psalm 119:103 -- How sweet are thy words unto my taste! yea, sweeter than honey to my mouth!

Psalm 119:116 -- Uphold me according unto thy word, that I may live: and let me not be ashamed of my hope.

Psalm 119:133 -- Order my steps in thy word: and let not any iniquity have dominion over me.

Psalm 119:140 -- Thy word is very pure: therefore thy servant loveth it.

Psalm 119:154 -- Plead my cause, and deliver me: quicken me according to thy word.

Psalm 119:170 -- Let my supplication come before thee: deliver me according to thy word.

Psalm 119:67 -- Before I was afflicted I went astray: but now have I kept thy word.

Psalm 138:2 -- I will worship toward thy holy temple, and praise thy name for thy lovingkindness and for thy truth: for thou hast magnified thy word above all thy name.

Revelations 12:11 -- And they overcame him by the blood of the Lamb, and by the word of their testimony; and they loved not their lives unto the death.

Romans 10:17 -- So then faith cometh by hearing, and hearing by the word of God.

Romans 12:1 -- I beseech you therefore, brethren, by the mercies of God, that ye present your bodies a living sacrifice, holy, acceptable unto God, which is your reasonable service.

Titus 1:9 -- Holding fast the faithful word as he hath been taught, that he may be able by sound doctrine both to exhort and to convince the gainsayers.

Know and Do God's Work
Labor
1 Corinthians 3:9 -- For we are labourers together with God: ye are God's husbandry, ye are God's building.

1 Corinthians 15:58 -- Therefore, my beloved brethren, be ye steadfast, unmoveable, always abounding in the work of the Lord, forasmuch as ye know that your labour is not in vain in the Lord.

1 Timothy 5:8 -- But if any provide not for his own, and specially for those of his own house, he hath denied the faith, and is worse than an infidel.

2 Corinthians 5:9 -- Wherefore we labour, that, whether present or absent, we may be accepted of him.

2 Timothy 2:15 -- Study to shew thyself approved unto God, a workman that needeth not to be ashamed, rightly dividing the word of truth.

Acts 20:35 -- I have shewed you all things, how that so labouring ye ought to support the weak, and to remember the words of the Lord Jesus, how he said, It is more blessed to give than to receive.

Colossians 1:10 -- That ye might walk worthy of the Lord unto all pleasing, being fruitful in every good work, and increasing in the knowledge of God;

Ecclesiastes 4:9 -- Two are better than one; because they have a good reward for their labour.

Ecclesiastes 5:19 -- Every man also to whom God hath given riches and wealth, and hath given him power to eat thereof, and to take his portion, and to rejoice in his labour; this is the gift of God.

John 6:27 -- Labour not for the meat which perisheth, but for that meat which endureth unto everlasting life, which the Son of man shall give unto you: for him hath God the Father sealed.

Joshua 24:13 -- And I have given you a land for which ye did not labour, and cities which ye built not, and ye dwell in them; of the vineyards and oliveyards which ye planted not do ye eat.

Matthew 11:28 -- Come unto me, all ye that labour and are heavy laden, and I will give you rest.

Psalm 127:1 -- A Song of degrees for Solomon. Except the LORD build the house, they labour in vain that build it: except the LORD keep the city, the watchman waketh but in vain.

Psalm 128:2 -- For thou shalt eat the labour of thine hands: happy shalt thou be, and it shall be well with thee.

Putting God First
Matthew 6:33 -- *But seek ye first the kingdom of God,*
and his righteousness; and all these things shall be added unto you.

1 Corinthians 7:20-24 -- Let every man abide in the same calling wherein he was called. Art thou called being a servant? care not for it: but if thou mayest be made free, use it rather. For he that is called in the Lord, being a servant, is the Lord's freeman: likewise also he that is called, being free, is Christ's servant. Ye are bought with a price; be not ye the servants of men. Brethren, let every man, wherein he is called, therein abide with God.

2 Corinthians 5:17 -- Therefore if any man be in Christ, he is a new creature: old things are passed away; behold, all things are become new.

Deuteronomy 28:1 -- And it shall come to pass, if thou shalt hearken diligently unto the voice of the LORD thy God, to observe and to do all his commandments which I command thee this day, that the LORD thy God will set thee on high above all nations of the earth:

Proverbs 8:33-34 -- Hear instruction, and be wise, and refuse it not. Blessed is the man that heareth me, watching daily at my gates, waiting at the posts of my doors.

Psalm 128:4 -- Behold, that thus shall the man be blessed that feareth the LORD.

Thanksgiving/ Praise
Psalm 116:17 -- *I will offer to thee the sacrifice*
of thanksgiving, and will call upon the name of the LORD.

Worship
John 4:24 -- *God is a Spirit: and they that worship*
him must worship him in spirit and in truth.

1 Corinthians 15:57 -- But thanks be to God, which giveth us the victory through our Lord Jesus Christ.

1 Timothy 2:1 -- I exhort therefore, that, first of all, supplications, prayers, intercessions, and giving of thanks, be made for all men;

Hebrews 13:15 -- By him therefore let us offer the sacrifice of praise to God continually, that is, the fruit of our lips giving thanks to his name.

Isaiah 12:2 -- Behold, God is my salvation; I will trust, and not be afraid: for the LORD JEHOVAH is my strength and my song; he also is become my salvation.

John 2:9 -- But I will sacrifice unto thee with the voice of thanksgiving; I will pay that that I have vowed. Salvation is of the LORD.

John 4:23 -- But the hour cometh, and now is, when the true worshippers shall worship the Father in spirit and in truth: for the Father seeketh such to worship him.

Philippians 4:6 -- Be careful for nothing; but in every thing by prayer and supplication with thanksgiving let your requests be made known unto God.

Psalm 100:4 -- Enter into his gates with thanksgiving, and into his courts with praise: be thankful unto him, and bless his name.

Psalm 34:2-3 -- My soul shall make her boast in the LORD: the humble shall hear thereof, and be glad. O magnify the LORD with me, and let us exalt his name together.

Psalm 50:14 -- Offer unto God thanksgiving; and pay thy vows unto the most High:

Psalm 69:30 -- I will praise the name of God with a song, and will magnify him with thanksgiving.

Psalm 95:1-3 -- O come, let us sing unto the LORD: let us make a joyful noise to the rock of our salvation. Let us come before his presence with thanksgiving, and make a joyful noise unto him with

Psalm. For the LORD is a great God, and a great King above all gods. Psalm 95:6-7 -- O come, let us worship and bow down: let us kneel before the LORD our maker. For he is our God; and we are the people of his pasture, and the sheep of his hand. To day if ye will hear his voice,

Revelations 15:4 -- Who shall not fear thee, O Lord, and glorify thy name? for thou only art holy: for all nations shall come and worship before thee; for thy judgments are made manifest.

Revelations 4:11 -- Thou art worthy, O Lord, to receive glory and honour and power: for thou hast created all things, and for thy pleasure they are and were created.

Revelations 7:12b -- Blessing, and glory, and wisdom, and thanksgiving, and honour, and power, and might, be unto our God for ever and ever. Amen.

Serving the Lord

John 12:26 -- If any man serve me, let him follow me;
and where I am, there shall also my servant be:
if any man serve me, him will my Father honour:

Acts 27:23 -- For there stood by me this night the angel of God, whose I am, and whom I serve,

Isaiah 56:7 -- Even them will I bring to my holy mountain, and make them joyful in my house of prayer: their burnt offerings and their sacrifices shall be accepted upon mine altar; for mine house shall be called an house of prayer for all people.

Luke 16:13 -- No servant can serve two masters: for either he will hate the one, and love the other; or else he will hold to the one, and despise the other. Ye cannot serve God and mammon.

Psalm 101:6 -- Mine eyes shall be upon the faithful of the land, that they may dwell with me: he that walketh in a perfect way, he shall serve me.

Romans 12:1 -- I beseech you therefore, brethren, by the mercies of God, that ye present your bodies a living sacrifice, holy, acceptable unto God, which is your reasonable service.

Zephaniah 3:9 -- For then will I turn to the people a pure language, that they may all call upon the name of the LORD, to serve him with one consent.

Deliverance

Jeremiah 33:3 -- *Call unto me, and I will answer thee, and shew thee great and mighty things, which thou knowest not.*

Isaiah 30:21 -- And thine ears shall hear a word behind thee, saying, This is the way, walk ye in it, when ye turn to the right hand, and when ye turn to the left.

Isaiah 54:14 -- In righteousness shalt thou be established: thou shalt be far from oppression; for thou shalt not fear: and from terror; for it shall not come near thee.

Isaiah 54:17 -- No weapon that is formed against thee shall prosper; and every tongue that shall rise against thee in judgment thou shalt condemn. This is the heritage of the servants of the LORD, and their righteousness is of me, saith the LORD.

Joel 2:32 -- And it shall come to pass, that whosoever shall call on the name of the LORD shall be delivered: for in mount Zion and in Jerusalem shall be deliverance, as the LORD hath said, and in the remnant whom the LORD shall call.

Proverbs 3:5-6 -- Trust in the LORD with all thine heart; and lean not unto thine own understanding. In all thy ways acknowledge him, and he shall direct thy paths.

Psalm 18:30 -- As for God, his way is perfect: the word of the LORD is tried: he is a buckler to all those that trust in him.

Psalm 32:7-8 -- Thou art my hiding place; thou shalt preserve me from trouble; thou shalt compass me about with songs of deliverance. Selah. I will instruct thee and teach thee in the way which thou shalt go: I will guide thee with mine eye.

Psalm 36:9 -- For with thee is the fountain of life: in thy light shall we see light.

Psalm 43:3 -- O send out thy light and thy truth: let them lead me; let them bring me unto thy holy hill, and to thy tabernacles.

Restoration
Psalm 51:12 -- *Restore unto me the joy of thy salvation;*
and uphold me with thy free spirit.

Isaiah 58:12 -- And they that shall be of thee shall build the old waste places: thou shalt raise up the foundations of many generations; and thou shalt be called, The repairer of the breach, The restorer of paths to dwell in.

Jeremiah 30:17 -- For I will restore health unto thee, and I will heal thee of thy wounds, saith the LORD; because they called thee an Outcast, saying, This is Zion, whom no man seeketh after.

Psalm 23:3 -- He restoreth my soul: he leadeth me in the paths of righteousness for his name's sake.

The Inner Life
3 John 1:2 -- *Beloved, I wish above all things that thou*
mayest prosper and be in health, even as thy soul prospereth.

1 Corinthians 4:2 -- Moreover it is required in stewards, that a man be found faithful.

1 Corinthians 15:58 -- Therefore, my beloved brethren, be ye stedfast, unmoveable, always abounding in the work of the Lord, forasmuch as ye know that your labour is not in vain in the Lord.

Colossians 3:17 -- And whatsoever ye do in word or deed, do all in the name of the Lord Jesus, giving thanks to God and the Father by him.

Galatians 6:2 -- Bear ye one another's burdens, and so fulfil the law of Christ.

John 13:34 -- A new commandment I give unto you, That ye love one another; as I have loved you, that ye also love one another.

Luke 6:45 -- A good man out of the good treasure of his heart bringeth forth that which is good; and an evil man out of the evil treasure of his heart bringeth forth that which is evil: for of the abundance of the heart his mouth speaketh.

Proverbs 13:20 -- He that walketh with wise men shall be wise: but a companion of fools shall be destroyed.

Psalm 4:8 -- I will both lay me down in peace, and sleep: for thou, LORD, only makest me dwell in safety.

Psalm 85:8 -- I will hear what God the LORD will speak: for he will speak peace unto his people, and to his saints: but let them not turn again to folly.

Romans 12:1-2 -- I beseech you therefore, brethren, by the mercies of God, that ye present your bodies a living sacrifice, holy, acceptable unto God, which is your reasonable service. And be not conformed to this world: but be ye transformed by the renewing of your mind, that ye may prove what is that good, and acceptable, and perfect, will of God.

Romans 15:5-7 -- Now the God of patience and consolation grant you to be likeminded one toward another according to Christ Jesus: That ye may with one mind and one mouth glorify God, even the Father of our Lord Jesus Christ. Wherefore receive ye one another, as Christ also received us to the glory of God.

Consecration

1 Peter 2:9 -- *But ye are a chosen generation, a royal priesthood, an holy nation, a peculiar people; that ye should shew forth the praises of him who hath called you out of darkness into his marvellous light:*

1 John 1:7 -- But if we walk in the light, as he is in the light, we have fellowship one with another, and the blood of Jesus Christ his Son cleanseth us from all sin.

1 John 1:9 -- If we confess our sins, he is faithful and just to forgive us our sins, and to cleanse us from all unrighteousness.

Psalm 15:1-2 -- A Psalm of David. LORD, who shall abide in thy tabernacle? who shall dwell in thy holy hill? He that walketh uprightly, and worketh righteousness, and speaketh the truth in his heart.

Romans 12:1-2 -- I beseech you therefore, brethren, by the mercies of God, that ye present your bodies a living sacrifice, holy, acceptable unto God, which is your reasonable service. And be not conformed to this world: but be ye transformed by the renewing of your mind, that ye may prove what is that good, and acceptable, and perfect, will of God.

Growth

2 Peter 3:18 -- But grow in grace, and in the knowledge
of our Lord and Saviour Jesus Christ.
To him be glory both now and for ever. Amen.

1 Peter 2:2 -- As newborn babes, desire the sincere milk of the word, that ye may grow thereby:

Hosea 14:7 -- They that dwell under his shadow shall return; they shall revive as the corn, and grow as the vine: the scent thereof shall be as the wine of Lebanon.

Malachi 4:2 -- But unto you that fear my name shall the Sun of righteousness arise with healing in his wings; and ye shall go forth, and grow up as calves of the stall.

Psalm 92:12 -- The righteous shall flourish like the palm tree: he shall grow like a cedar in Lebanon.

Strength

Psalm 118:14 -- The LORD is my strength and song,
and is become my salvation.

1 Corinthians 15:57 -- But thanks be to God, which giveth us the victory through our Lord Jesus Christ.

1 John 5:4 -- For whatsoever is born of God overcometh the world: and this is the victory that overcometh the world, even our faith.

2 Chronicles 15:7 -- Be ye strong therefore, and let not your hands be weak: for your work shall be rewarded.

2 Corinthians 12:9-10 -- And he said unto me, My grace is sufficient for thee: for my strength is made perfect in weakness. Most gladly therefore will I rather glory in my infirmities, that the power of Christ may rest upon me. Therefore I take pleasure in infirmities, in reproaches, in necessities, in persecutions, in distresses for Christ's sake: for when I am weak, then am I strong.

2 Samuel 22:33 -- God is my strength and power: and he maketh my way perfect.

Ephesians 6:10 -- Finally, my brethren, be strong in the Lord, and in the power of his might.

Exodus 15:2 -- The LORD is my strength and song, and he is become my salvation: he is my God, and I will prepare him an habitation; my father's God, and I will exalt him.

Isaiah 30:15 -- For thus saith the Lord GOD, the Holy One of Israel; In returning and rest shall ye be saved; in quietness and in confidence shall be your strength: and ye would not.

Isaiah 41:10 -- Fear thou not; for I am with thee: be not dismayed; for I am thy God: I will strengthen thee; yea, I will help thee; yea, I will uphold thee with the right hand of my righteousness.

Job 4:3-4 -- Behold, thou hast instructed many, and thou hast strengthened the weak hands. Thy words have upholden him that was falling, and thou hast strengthened the feeble knees.

Proverbs 24:5 -- A wise man is strong; yea, a man of knowledge increaseth strength.

Psalm 22:19 -- But be not thou far from me, O LORD: O my strength, haste thee to help me.

Psalm 28:7 -- The LORD is my strength and my shield; my heart trusted in him, and I am helped: therefore my heart greatly rejoiceth; and with my song will I praise him.

Psalm 31:4 -- Pull me out of the net that they have laid privily for me: for thou art my strength.

Psalm 37:39 -- But the salvation of the righteous is of the LORD: he is their strength in the time of trouble.

Psalm 84:5 -- Blessed is the man whose strength is in thee; in whose heart are the ways of them.

Psalm 147:13 -- For he hath strengthened the bars of thy gates; he hath blessed thy children within thee.

Trust
Psalm 9:10 -- And they that know thy name
will put their trust in thee: for thou,
LORD, hast not forsaken them that seek thee.

Isaiah 12:2 -- Behold, God is my salvation; I will trust, and not be afraid: for the LORD JEHOVAH is my strength and my song; he also is become my salvation.

Job 13:15 -- Though he slay me, yet will I trust in him: but I will maintain mine own ways before him.

Proverbs 16:20 -- He that handleth a matter wisely shall find good: and whoso trusteth in the LORD, happy is he.

Proverbs 28:26 -- He that trusteth in his own heart is a fool: but whoso walketh wisely, he shall be delivered.

Proverbs 3:5 -- Trust in the LORD with all thine heart; and lean not unto thine own understanding.

Psalm 22:4 -- Our fathers trusted in thee: they trusted, and thou didst deliver them.

Psalm 25:2 -- O my God, I trust in thee: let me not be ashamed, let not mine enemies triumph over me.

Psalm 28:7 -- The LORD is my strength and my shield; my heart trusted in him, and I am helped: therefore my heart greatly rejoiceth; and with my song will I praise him.

Psalm 37:3 -- Trust in the LORD, and do good; so shalt thou dwell in the land, and verily thou shalt be fed.

Psalm 56:3 -- What time I am afraid, I will trust in thee.

Psalm 62:8 -- Trust in him at all times; ye people, pour out your heart before him: God is a refuge for us. Selah.

Psalm 86:2 -- Preserve my soul; for I am holy: O thou my God, save thy servant that trusteth in thee.

Psalm 91:4 -- He shall cover thee with his feathers, and under his wings shalt thou trust: his truth shall be thy shield and buckler.

Psalm 112:7 -- He shall not be afraid of evil tidings: his heart is fixed, trusting in the LORD.

Psalm 143:8 -- Cause me to hear thy lovingkindness in the morning; for in thee do I trust: cause me to know the way wherein I should walk; for I lift up my soul unto thee.

Forgiveness
Ephesians 4:32 -- And be ye kind one to another,
tenderhearted, forgiving one another,
even as God for Christ's sake hath forgiven you.

1 John 1:9 -- If we confess our sins, he is faithful and just to forgive us our sins, and to cleanse us from all unrighteousness.

1 John 2:12 -- I write unto you, little children, because your sins are forgiven you for his name's sake.

Colossians 1:14 -- In whom we have redemption through his blood, even the forgiveness of sins:

Colossians 2:13 -- And you, being dead in your sins and the uncircumcision of your flesh, hath he quickened together with him, having forgiven you all trespasses;

Ephesians 1:7 -- In whom we have redemption through his blood, the forgiveness of sins, according to the riches of his grace;

James 5:15 -- And the prayer of faith shall save the sick, and the Lord shall raise him up; and if he have committed sins, they shall be forgiven him.

Luke 11:4 -- And forgive us our sins; for we also forgive every one that is indebted to us. And lead us not into temptation; but deliver us from evil.

Mark 11:25 -- And when ye stand praying, forgive, if ye have ought against any: that your Father also which is in heaven may forgive you your trespasses.

Matthew 6:12 -- And forgive us our debts, as we forgive our debtors.

Psalm 32:1 -- A Psalm of David, Maschil. Blessed is he whose transgression is forgiven, whose sin is covered.

Psalm 32:5 -- I acknowledged my sin unto thee, and mine iniquity have I not hid. I said, I will confess my transgressions unto the LORD; and thou forgavest the iniquity of my sin. Selah.

Romans 12:14 -- Bless them which persecute you: bless, and curse not.

Resisting Satan's Lies
1 Corinthians 6:20 -- *For ye are bought with a price:*
therefore glorify God in your body,
and in your spirit, which are God's.

1 Peter 1:13 -- Wherefore gird up the loins of your mind, be sober, and hope to the end for the grace that is to be brought unto you at the revelation of Jesus Christ;

2 Corinthians 10:3-5 -- For though we walk in the flesh, we do not war after the flesh: (For the weapons of our warfare are not carnal, but mighty through God to the pulling down of strong holds;) Casting down imaginations, and every high thing that exalteth itself against the knowledge of God, and bringing into captivity every thought to the obedience of Christ;

Colossians 3:2 -- Set your affection on things above, not on things on the earth.

Philippians 4:8-9 -- Finally, brethren, whatsoever things are true, whatsoever things are honest, whatsoever things are just, whatsoever things are pure, whatsoever things are lovely, whatsoever things are of good report; if there be any virtue, and if there be any praise, think on these things. Those things, which ye have both learned, and received, and heard, and seen in me, do: and the God of peace shall be with you.

Faith

Romans 10:17 -- So then faith cometh by hearing,
and hearing by the word of God.

1 John 5:4 -- For whatsoever is born of God overcometh the world: and this is the victory that overcometh the world, even our faith.

1 Peter 1:7 -- That the trial of your faith, being much more precious than of gold that perisheth, though it be tried with fire, might be found unto praise and honour and glory at the appearing of Jesus Christ:

1 Peter 5:9 -- Whom resist steadfast in the faith, knowing that the same afflictions are accomplished in your brethren that are in the world.

2 Corinthians 5:7 -- For we walk by faith, not by sight:

Galatians 3:11 -- But that no man is justified by the law in the sight of God, it is evident: for, The just shall live by faith.

Hebrews 10:23 -- Let us hold fast the profession of our faith without wavering; (for he is faithful that promised;)

Jude 1:3 -- Beloved, when I gave all diligence to write unto you of the common salvation, it was needful for me to write unto you, and exhort you that ye should earnestly contend for the faith which was once delivered unto the saints.

Matthew 17:20 -- And Jesus said unto them, Because of your unbelief: for verily I say unto you, If ye have faith as a grain of mustard seed, ye shall say unto this mountain, Remove hence to yonder place; and it shall remove; and nothing shall be impossible unto you.

Proverbs 28:20 -- A faithful man shall abound with blessings: but he that maketh haste to be rich shall not be innocent.

Romans 12:3 -- For I say, through the grace given unto me, to every man that is among you, not to think of himself more highly than he ought to think; but to think soberly, according as God hath dealt to every man the measure of faith.

Fruit of the Spirit

Ephesians 4:23-24 -- *And be renewed in the spirit of your mind; And that ye put on the new man, which after God is created in righteousness and true holiness.*

1 Timothy 6:11 -- But thou, O man of God, flee these things; and follow after righteousness, godliness, faith, love, patience, meekness.

2 Peter 1:5 -- And beside this, giving all diligence, add to your faith virtue; and to virtue knowledge;

2 Peter 1:6 -- And to knowledge temperance; and to temperance patience; and to patience godliness;

2 Timothy 1:7 -- For God hath not given us the spirit of fear; but of power, and of love, and of a sound mind.

Ephesians 4:1-2 -- I therefore, the prisoner of the Lord, beseech you that ye walk worthy of the vocation wherewith ye are called, With all lowliness and meekness, with longsuffering, forbearing one another in love;

Ephesians 4:7 -- But unto every one of us is given grace according to the measure of the gift of Christ.

Ephesians 4:22 -- That ye put off concerning the former conversation the old man, which is corrupt according to the deceitful lusts;

Ephesians 4:25-32 -- Wherefore putting away lying, speak every man truth with his neighbour: for we are members one of another. Be ye angry, and sin not: let not the sun go down upon your wrath: Neither give place to the devil. Let him that stole steal no more: but rather let him labour, working with his hands the thing which is good, that he may have to give to him that needeth. Let no corrupt communication proceed out of your mouth, but that which is good to the use of edifying, that it may minister grace unto the hearers. And grieve not the holy Spirit of God, whereby ye are sealed unto the day of redemption. Let all bitterness, and wrath, and anger, and clamour, and evil speaking, be put away from you, with all malice: And be ye kind one to another, tenderhearted, forgiving one another, even as God for Christ's sake hath forgiven you.

Galatians 5:16 -- This I say then, Walk in the Spirit, and ye shall not fulfil the lust of the flesh.

Galatians 5:24 -- And they that are Christ's have crucified the flesh with the affections and lusts.

Luke 8:15 -- But that on the good ground are they, which in an honest and good heart, having heard the word, keep it, and bring forth fruit with patience.

Philippians 4:7 -- And the peace of God, which passeth all understanding, shall keep your hearts and minds through Christ Jesus.

Proverbs 16:32 -- He that is slow to anger is better than the mighty; and he that ruleth his spirit than he that taketh a city.

Psalm 37:7-9 -- Rest in the LORD, and wait patiently for him: fret not thyself because of him who prospereth in his way, because of the man who bringeth wicked devices to pass. Cease from anger, and forsake wrath: fret not thyself in any wise to do evil. For evildoers shall be cut off: but those that wait upon the LORD, they shall inherit the earth.

Psalm 119:165 -- Great peace have they which love thy law: and nothing shall offend them.

Romans 13:14 -- But put ye on the Lord Jesus Christ, and make not provision for the flesh, to fulfil the lusts thereof.

Romans 14:17 -- For the kingdom of God is not meat and drink; but righteousness, and peace, and joy in the Holy Ghost.

Romans 5:3 -- And not only so, but we glory in tribulations also: knowing that tribulation worketh patience;

Romans 6:6 -- Knowing this, that our old man is crucified with him, that the body of sin might be destroyed, that henceforth we should not serve sin.

Knowledge

Isaiah 11:2 -- *And the spirit of the LORD shall rest upon him, the spirit of wisdom and understanding, the spirit of counsel and might, the spirit of knowledge and of the fear of the LORD;*

1 John 2:27 -- But the anointing which ye have received of him abideth in you, and ye need not that any man teach you: but as the same anointing teacheth you of all things, and is truth, and is no lie, and even as it hath taught you, ye shall abide in him.

Daniel 2:21 -- And he changeth the times and the seasons: he removeth kings, and setteth up kings: he giveth wisdom unto the wise, and knowledge to them that know understanding:

Exodus 31:3 -- And I have filled him with the spirit of God, in wisdom, and in understanding, and in knowledge, and in all manner of workmanship,

James 3:13 -- Who is a wise man and endued with knowledge among you? let him shew out of a good conversation his works with meekness of wisdom.

Job 36:3 -- I will fetch my knowledge from afar, and will ascribe righteousness to my Maker.

Malachi 2:7 -- For the priest's lips should keep knowledge, and they should seek the law at his mouth: for he is the messenger of the LORD of hosts.

Proverbs 1:7 -- The fear of the LORD is the beginning of knowledge: but fools despise wisdom and instruction.

Proverbs 8:10 -- Receive my instruction, and not silver; and knowledge rather than choice gold.

Proverbs 12:1 -- Whoso loveth instruction loveth knowledge: but he that hateth reproof is brutish.

Proverbs 15:7 -- The lips of the wise disperse knowledge: but the heart of the foolish doeth not so.

Wisdom

Isaiah 33:6 -- And wisdom and knowledge shall be the stability of thy times, and strength of salvation: the fear of the LORD is his treasure.

Ephesians 1:17-19 -- That the God of our Lord Jesus Christ, the Father of glory, may give unto you the spirit of wisdom and revelation in the knowledge of him: The eyes of your understanding being enlightened; that ye may know what is the hope of his calling, and what the riches of the glory of his inheritance in the saints, And what is the exceeding greatness of his power to us-ward who believe, according to the working of his mighty power,

Proverbs 1:7 -- The fear of the LORD is the beginning of knowledge: but fools despise wisdom and instruction.

Proverbs 2:2 -- So that thou incline thine ear unto wisdom, and apply thine heart to understanding;

Psalm 37:30 -- The mouth of the righteous speaketh wisdom, and his tongue talketh of judgment.

Understanding
Job 32:8 -- But there is a spirit in man: and the inspiration of the Almighty giveth them understanding.

1 John 5:20 -- And we know that the Son of God is come, and hath given us an understanding, that we may know him that is true, and we are in him that is true, even in his Son Jesus Christ. This is the true God, and eternal life.

Ephesians 5:17 -- Wherefore be ye not unwise, but understanding what the will of the Lord is.

Exodus 31:3 -- And I have filled him with the spirit of God, in wisdom, and in understanding, and in knowledge, and in all manner of workmanship,

Proverbs 4:7 -- Wisdom is the principal thing; therefore get wisdom: and with all thy getting get understanding.

Proverbs 7:4 -- Say unto wisdom, Thou art my sister; and call understanding thy kinswoman:

Proverbs 8:9 -- They are all plain to him that understandeth, and right to them that find knowledge.

Psalm 111:10 -- The fear of the LORD is the beginning of wisdom: a good understanding have all they that do his commandments: his praise endureth for ever.

Psalm 119:34 -- Give me understanding, and I shall keep thy law; yea, I shall observe it with my whole heart.

Psalm 119:130 -- The entrance of thy words giveth light; it giveth understanding unto the simple.

Confidence
Proverbs 14:26 -- In the fear of the LORD is strong confidence: and his children shall have a place of refuge.

2 Corinthians 5:8 -- We are confident, I say, and willing rather to be absent from the body, and to be present with the Lord.

Ephesians 3:12 -- In whom we have boldness and access with confidence by the faith of him.

Hebrews 3:6 -- But Christ as a son over his own house; whose house are we, if we hold fast the confidence and the rejoicing of the hope firm unto the end.

Matthew 10:32 -- Whosoever therefore shall confess me before men, him will I confess also before my Father which is in heaven.

Philippians 1:6 -- Being confident of this very thing, that he whi hath begun a good work in you will perform it until the day of Jesus Christ:

Philippians 4:13 -- I can do all things through Christ which strengtheneth me.

Proverbs 3:26 -- For the LORD shall be thy confidence, and sha keep thy foot from being taken.

Psalm 27:3 -- Though an host should encamp against me, my heart shall not fear: though war should rise against me, in this will I confident.

Psalm 118:8-9 -- It is better to trust in the LORD than to put confidence in man. It is better to trust in the LORD than to put confidence in princes.

Commitment

*Luke 9:23 -- And he said to them all, If any man will
come after me, let him deny himself, and take up
his cross daily, and follow me*

1 Corinthians 9:27 -- But I keep under my body, and bring it i subjection: lest that by any means, when I have preached to others myself should be a castaway.

2 Timothy 1:12 -- For the which cause I also suffer these thin nevertheless I am not ashamed: for I know whom I have believed, am persuaded that he is able to keep that which I have committed him against that day.

Luke 9:24 -- For whosoever will save his life shall lose it: bu whosoever will lose his life for my sake, the same shall save it.

Luke 9:25 -- For what is a man advantaged, if he gain the wl world, and lose himself, or be cast away?

Matthew 10:22 -- And ye shall be hated of all men for my na sake: but he that endureth to the end shall be saved.

Matthew 7:7 -- Ask, and it shall be given you; seek, and ye : find; knock, and it shall be opened unto you:

Diligence

2 Peter 1:10 -- *Wherefore the rather, brethren,*
give diligence to make your calling and
election sure: for if ye do these things, ye shall never fall:

1 Corinthians 9:27 -- But I keep under my body, and bring it into subjection: lest that by any means, when I have preached to others, I myself should be a castaway.

1 Timothy 2:8 -- I will therefore that men pray every where, lifting up holy hands, without wrath and doubting.

2 Corinthians 8:7 -- Therefore, as ye abound in every thing, in faith, and utterance, and knowledge, and in all diligence, and in your love to us, see that ye abound in this grace also.

Deuteronomy 4:9 -- Only take heed to thyself, and keep thy soul diligently, lest thou forget the things which thine eyes have seen, and lest they depart from thy heart all the days of thy life: but teach them thy sons, and thy sons' sons;

Proverbs 10:4 -- He becometh poor that dealeth with a slack hand: but the hand of the diligent maketh rich.

Proverbs 12:24 -- The hand of the diligent shall bear rule: but the slothful shall be under tribute.

Proverbs 21:5 -- The thoughts of the diligent tend only to plenteousness; but of every one that is hasty only to want.

Proverbs 22:29 -- Seest thou a man diligent in his business? he shall stand before kings; he shall not stand before mean men.

Proverbs 27:23 -- Be thou diligent to know the state of thy flocks, and look well to thy herds.

Proverbs 4:23 -- Keep thy heart with all diligence; for out of it are the issues of life.

Romans 12:11 -- Not slothful in business; fervent in spirit; serving the Lord;

Growth / Acceleration

Ephesians 3:20 -- *Now unto him that is able to do exceeding abundantly above all that we ask or think, according to the power that worketh in us,*

Elevation

Psalm 37:34 -- *Wait on the LORD, and keep his way, and he shall exalt thee to inherit the land: when the wicked are cut off, thou shalt see it.*

1 Peter 5:6 -- Humble yourselves therefore under the mighty hand of God, that he may exalt you in due time:

1 Samuel 2:10 -- The adversaries of the LORD shall be broken to pieces; out of heaven shall he thunder upon them: the LORD shall judge the ends of the earth; and he shall give strength unto his king, and exalt the horn of his anointed.

Acts 13:17 -- The God of this people of Israel chose our fathers, and exalted the people when they dwelt as strangers in the land of Egypt, and with an high arm brought he them out of it.

Genesis 17:2 -- And I will make my covenant between me and thee, and will multiply thee exceedingly.

Genesis 17:6 -- And I will make thee exceeding fruitful, and I will make nations of thee, and kings shall come out of thee.

Isaiah 30:18 -- And therefore will the LORD wait, that he may be gracious unto you, and therefore will he be exalted, that he may have mercy upon you: for the LORD is a God of judgment: blessed are all they that wait for him.

James 1:9 -- Let the brother of low degree rejoice in that he is exalted:

Job 5:11 -- To set up on high those that be low; that those which mourn may be exalted to safety.

Matthew 23:12 -- And whosoever shall exalt himself shall be abased; and he that shall humble himself shall be exalted.

Psalm 89:17 -- For thou art the glory of their strength: and in thy favour our horn shall be exalted.

Perseverance / Patience

James 1:4 -- *But let patience have her perfect work,*
that ye may be perfect and entire, wanting nothing.

1 Peter 5:10 -- But the God of all grace, who hath called us unto his eternal glory by Christ Jesus, after that ye have suffered a while, make you perfect, stablish, strengthen, settle you.

2 Timothy 2:10 -- Therefore I endure all things for the elect's sakes, that they may also obtain the salvation which is in Christ Jesus with eternal glory.

2 Timothy 2:24 -- And the servant of the Lord must not strive; but be gentle unto all men, apt to teach, patient,

Ecclesiastes 7:8 -- Better is the end of a thing than the beginning thereof: and the patient in spirit is better than the proud in spirit.

Hebrews 10:36 -- For ye have need of patience, that, after ye have done the will of God, ye might receive the promise.

Hebrews 12:1 -- Wherefore seeing we also are compassed about with so great a cloud of witnesses, let us lay aside every weight, and the sin which doth so easily beset us, and let us run with patience the race that is set before us,

Hebrews 6:12 -- That ye be not slothful, but followers of them who through faith and patience inherit the promises.

Hebrews 6:15 -- And so, after he had patiently endured, he obtained the promise.

James 1:12 -- Blessed is the man that endureth temptation: for when he is tried, he shall receive the crown of life, which the Lord hath promised to them that love him.

James 1:3 -- Knowing this, that the trying of your faith worketh patience.

James 5:7 -- Be patient therefore, brethren, unto the coming of the Lord. Behold, the husbandman waiteth for the precious fruit of the earth, and hath long patience for it, until he receive the early and latter rain.

James 5:8 -- Be ye also patient; stablish your hearts: for the coming of the Lord draweth nigh.

Luke 21:19 -- In your patience possess ye your souls.

Luke 8:15 -- But that on the good ground are they, which in an honest and good heart, having heard the word, keep it, and bring forth fruit with patience.

Romans 5:3-4 -- And not only so, but we glory in tribulations also: knowing that tribulation worketh patience; And patience, experience; and experience, hope:

Romans 8:25 -- But if we hope for that we see not, then do we with patience wait for it.

Romans 12:12 -- Rejoicing in hope; patient in tribulation; continuing instant in prayer;

Romans 15:4-5 -- For whatsoever things were written aforetime were written for our learning, that we through patience and comfort of the scriptures might have hope. Now the God of patience and consolation grant you to be likeminded one toward another according to Christ Jesus:

Titus 2:2 -- That the aged men be sober, grave, temperate, sound in faith, in charity, in patience.

Steadfastness

Revelations 3:11 -- *Behold, I come quickly: hold that fast which thou hast, that no man take thy crown.*

1 Corinthians 15:58 -- Therefore, my beloved brethren, be ye stedfast, unmoveable, always abounding in the work of the Lord, forasmuch as ye know that your labour is not in vain in the Lord.

1 Timothy 6:12 -- Fight the good fight of faith, lay hold on eternal life, whereunto thou art also called, and hast professed a good profession before many witnesses.

Hebrews 3:14 -- For we are made partakers of Christ, if we hold the beginning of our confidence stedfast unto the end;

Hebrews 6:19 -- Which hope we have as an anchor of the soul, both sure and stedfast, and which entereth into that within the veil;

Job 11:15 -- For then shalt thou lift up thy face without spot; yea, thou shalt be stedfast, and shalt not fear:

Victory

*1 John 4:4 -- Ye are of God, little children, and have
overcome them: because greater is he that is in you,
than he that is in the world.*

1 Corinthians 15:55 -- O death, where is thy sting? O grave, where
is thy victory?

1 John 5:4 -- For whatsoever is born of God overcometh the
world: and this is the victory that overcometh the world, even our faith.

1 Peter 4:10-11 -- As every man hath received the gift, even so
minister the same one to another, as good stewards of the manifold
grace of God. If any man speak, let him speak as the oracles of God; if
any man minister, let him do it as of the ability which God giveth: that
God in all things may be glorified through Jesus Christ, to whom be
praise and dominion for ever and ever. Amen.

2 Peter 1:3 -- According as his divine power hath given unto us all
things that pertain unto life and godliness, through the knowledge of
him that hath called us to glory and virtue:

Philippians 4:13 -- I can do all things through Christ which
strengtheneth me.

Psalm 18:29 -- For by thee I have run through a troop; and by my
God have I leaped over a wall.

Psalm 98:1 -- A Psalm. O sing unto the LORD a new song; for he
hath done marvellous things: his right hand, and his holy arm, hath
gotten him the victory.

Psalm 126:1 -- A Song of degrees. When the LORD turned again
the captivity of Zion, we were like them that dream.

Psalm 144:1 -- A Psalm of David. Blessed be the LORD my
strength, which teacheth my hands to war, and my fingers to fight:

Revelations 2:26 -- And he that overcometh, and keepeth my
works unto the end, to him will I give power over the nations:

Romans 8:37 -- Nay, in all these things we are more than
conquerors through him that loved us.

Favour

Psalm 5:12 -- For thou, LORD, wilt bless the righteous;
with favour wilt thou compass him as with a shield.

Job 10:12 -- Thou hast granted me life and favour, and thy visitation hath preserved my spirit.

Job 33:26 -- He shall pray unto God, and he will be favourable unto him: and he shall see his face with joy: for he will render unto man his righteousness.

Psalm 30:5 -- For his anger endureth but a moment; in his favour is life: weeping may endure for a night, but joy cometh in the morning.

Psalm 41:11 -- By this I know that thou favourest me, because mine enemy doth not triumph over me.

Psalm 89:17 -- For thou art the glory of their strength: and in thy favour our horn shall be exalted.

Psalm 102:13 -- Thou shalt arise, and have mercy upon Zion: for the time to favour her, yea, the set time, is come.

Proverbs 3:4 -- So shalt thou find favour and good understanding in the sight of God and man.

Proverbs 22:1 -- A good name is rather to be chosen than great riches, and loving favour rather than silver and gold.

Isaiah 45:2-3 -- I will go before thee, and make the crooked places straight: I will break in pieces the gates of brass, and cut in sunder the bars of iron: And I will give thee the treasures of darkness, and hidden riches of secret places, that thou mayest know that I, the LORD, which call thee by thy name, am the God of Israel.

Isaiah 60:10 -- And the sons of strangers shall build up thy walls, and their kings shall minister unto thee: for in my wrath I smote thee, but in my favour have I had mercy on thee.

Matthew 6:4 -- That thine alms may be in secret: and thy Father which seeth in secret himself shall reward thee openly.

Matthew 6:6 -- But thou, when thou prayest, enter into thy closet, and when thou hast shut thy door, pray to thy Father which is in secret; and thy Father which seeth in secret shall reward thee openly.

Matthew 10:41 -- He that receiveth a prophet in the name of a prophet shall receive a prophet's reward; and he that receiveth a righteous man in the name of a righteous man shall receive a righteous man's reward.

Matthew 16:27 -- For the Son of man shall come in the glory of his Father with his angels; and then he shall reward every man according to his works.

Luke 6:23 -- Rejoice ye in that day, and leap for joy: for, behold, your reward is great in heaven: for in the like manner did their fathers unto the prophets.

Power
Isaiah 40:29 -- He giveth power to the faint; and to them that have no might he increaseth strength.

Acts 1:8 -- But ye shall receive power, after that the Holy Ghost is come upon you: and ye shall be witnesses unto me both in Jerusalem, and in all Judaea, and in Samaria, and unto the uttermost part of the earth.

Ephesians 3:20 -- Now unto him that is able to do exceeding abundantly above all that we ask or think, according to the power that worketh in us,

John 1:12 -- But as many as received him, to them gave he power to become the sons of God, even to them that believe on his name:

Mark 6:7 -- And he called unto him the twelve, and began to send them forth by two and two; and gave them power over unclean spirits;

Micah 3:8 -- But truly I am full of power by the spirit of the LORD, and of judgment, and of might, to declare unto Jacob his transgression, and to Israel his sin.

Zechariah 4:6 -- Then he answered and spake unto me, saying, This is the word of the LORD unto Zerubbabel, saying, Not by might, nor by power, but by my spirit, saith the LORD of hosts.

Spiritual Gifts
1 Corinthians 14:12 -- Even so ye, forasmuch as ye are zealous of spiritual gifts, seek that ye may excel to the edifying of the church.

1 Corinthians 1:7 -- So that ye come behind in no gift; waiting for the coming of our Lord Jesus Christ:

1 Corinthians 12:10 -- To another the working of miracles; to another prophecy; to another discerning of spirits; to another divers kinds of tongues; to another the interpretation of tongues:

1 Corinthians 12:31 -- But covet earnestly the best gifts: and yet shew I unto you a more excellent way.

1 Corinthians 12:8-9 -- For to one is given by the Spirit the word of wisdom; to another the word of knowledge by the same Spirit; To another faith by the same Spirit; to another the gifts of healing by the same Spirit;

1 Corinthians 13:2 -- And though I have the gift of prophecy, and understand all mysteries, and all knowledge; and though I have all faith, so that I could remove mountains, and have not charity, I am nothing.

1 Corinthians 14:1 -- Follow after charity, and desire spiritual gifts, but rather that ye may prophesy.

1 Timothy 4:14 -- Neglect not the gift that is in thee, which was given thee by prophecy, with the laying on of the hands of the presbytery.

2 Chronicles 15:7 -- Be ye strong therefore, and let not your hands be weak: for your work shall be rewarded.

2 Corinthians 12:9 -- And he said unto me, My grace is sufficient for thee: for my strength is made perfect in weakness. Most gladly therefore will I rather glory in my infirmities, that the power of Christ may rest upon me.

2 Corinthians 2:14 -- Now thanks be unto God, which always causeth us to triumph in Christ, and maketh manifest the savour of his knowledge by us in every place.

2 Corinthians 4:8 -- We are troubled on every side, yet not distressed; we are perplexed, but not in despair;

2 Corinthians 6:4 -- But in all things approving ourselves as the ministers of God, in much patience, in afflictions, in necessities, in distresses,

2 Corinthians 9:8 -- And God is able to make all grace abound toward you; that ye, always having all sufficiency in all things, may abound to every good work:

2 Timothy 1:6 -- Wherefore I put thee in remembrance that thou stir up the gift of God, which is in thee by the putting on of my hands.

Ephesians 3:20 -- Now unto him that is able to do exceeding abundantly above all that we ask or think, according to the power that worketh in us,

Ephesians 4:7 -- But unto every one of us is given grace according to the measure of the gift of Christ.

Habakkuk 3:19 -- The LORD God is my strength, and he will make my feet like hinds' feet, and he will make me to walk upon mine high places. To the chief singer on my stringed instruments.

Isaiah 41:10 -- Fear thou not; for I am with thee: be not dismayed; for I am thy God: I will strengthen thee; yea, I will help thee; yea, I will uphold thee with the right hand of my righteousness.

James 1:17 -- Every good gift and every perfect gift is from above, and cometh down from the Father of lights, with whom is no variableness, neither shadow of turning.

Job 8:7 -- Though thy beginning was small, yet thy latter end should greatly increase.

Proverbs 18:16 -- A man's gift maketh room for him, and bringeth him before great men.

Romans 11:29 -- For the gifts and calling of God are without repentance.

Romans 12:6-7 -- Having then gifts differing according to the grace that is given to us, whether prophecy, let us prophesy according to the proportion of faith; Or ministry, let us wait on our ministering: or he that teacheth, on teaching;

Purpose
Romans 8:28 -- And we know that all things work together for good to them that love God, to them who are the called according to his purpose.

2 Corinthians 5:9 -- Wherefore we labour, that, whether present or absent, we may be accepted of him.

2 Timothy 3:10 -- But thou hast fully known my doctrine, manner of life, purpose, faith, longsuffering, charity, patience

Colossians 3:23 -- And whatsoever ye do, do it heartily, as to the Lord, and not unto men;

Ephesians 1:11 -- In whom also we have obtained an inheritance, being predestinated according to the purpose of him who worketh all things after the counsel of his own will:

Philippians 4:13 -- I can do all things through Christ which strengtheneth me.

Proverbs 15:22 -- Without counsel purposes are disappointed: but in the multitude of counselors they are established.

Romans 14:7-8 -- For none of us liveth to himself, and no man dieth to himself. For whether we live, we live unto the Lord; and whether we die, we die unto the Lord: whether we live therefore, or die, we are the Lord's.

Vision
Proverbs 29:18 -- Where there is no vision, the people perish: but he that keepeth the law, happy is he.

Habakkuk 2:2-3 -- And the LORD answered me, and said, Write the vision, and make it plain upon tables, that he may run that readeth it. For the vision is yet for an appointed time, but at the end it shall speak, and not lie: though it tarry, wait for it; because it will surely come, it will not tarry.

Joel 2:28 -- And it shall come to pass afterward, that I will pour out my spirit upon all flesh; and your sons and your daughters shall prophesy, your old men shall dream dreams, your young men shall see visions:

Psalm 92:11 -- Mine eye also shall see my desire on mine enemies, and mine ears shall hear my desire of the wicked that rise up against me.

Courage
Isaiah 41:6 -- They helped every one his neighbour; and every one said to his brother, Be of good courage.

1 Chronicles 28:20 -- And David said to Solomon his son, Be strong and of good courage, and do it: fear not, nor be dismayed: for the LORD God, even my God, will be with thee; he will not fail thee, nor forsake thee, until thou hast finished all the work for the service of the house of the LORD.

1 Corinthians 16:13 -- Watch ye, stand fast in the faith, quit you like men, be strong.

Deuteronomy 31:6 -- Be strong and of a good courage, fear not, nor be afraid of them: for the LORD thy God, he it is that doth go with thee; he will not fail thee, nor forsake thee.

Joshua 1:7 -- Only be thou strong and very courageous, that thou mayest observe to do according to all the law, which Moses my servant commanded thee: turn not from it to the right hand or to the left, that thou mayest prosper whithersoever thou goest.

Attainment / Possessing the Future

1 Peter 5:6 -- *Humble yourselves therefore under the mighty hand of God, that he may exalt you in due time:*

Colossians 3:23 -- And whatsoever ye do, do it heartily, as to the Lord, and not unto men;

Deuteronomy 8:18 -- But thou shalt remember the LORD thy God: for it is he that giveth thee power to get wealth, that he may establish his covenant which he sware unto thy fathers, as it is this day.

Hebrews 12:2 -- Looking unto Jesus the author and finisher of our faith; who for the joy that was set before him endured the cross, despising the shame, and is set down at the right hand of the throne of God.

Hebrews 13:5 -- Let your conversation be without covetousness; and be content with such things as ye have: for he hath said, I will never leave thee, nor forsake thee.

Isaiah 30:18 -- And therefore will the LORD wait, that he may be gracious unto you, and therefore will he be exalted, that he may have mercy upon you: for the LORD is a God of judgment: blessed are all they that wait for him.

James 1:9 -- Let the brother of low degree rejoice in that he is exalted:

John 14:14 -- If ye shall ask any thing in my name, I will do it.

Matthew 6:34 -- Take therefore no thought for the morrow: for the morrow shall take thought for the things of itself. Sufficient unto the day is the evil thereof.

Philippians 1:6 -- Being confident of this very thing, that he which hath begun a good work in you will perform it until the day of Jesus Christ:

Philippians 3:12 -- Not as though I had already attained, either were already perfect: but I follow after, if that I may apprehend that for which also I am apprehended of Christ Jesus.

Philippians 3:14 -- I press toward the mark for the prize of the high calling of God in Christ Jesus.

Philippians 3:16 -- Nevertheless, whereto we have already attained, let us walk by the same rule, let us mind the same thing.

Psalm 37:34 -- Wait on the LORD, and keep his way, and he shall exalt thee to inherit the land: when the wicked are cut off, thou shalt see it.

Psalm 89:17 -- For thou art the glory of their strength: and in thy favour our horn shall be exalted.

Psalm 112:9 -- He hath dispersed, he hath given to the poor; his righteousness endureth for ever; his horn shall be exalted with honour.

Romans 8:28 -- And we know that all things work together for good to them that love God, to them who are the called according to his purpose.

FAMILY

Husbands & Wives

1 Corinthians 7:3 -- *Let the husband render unto the wife due benevolence: and likewise also the wife unto the husband.*

1 Corinthians 7:2 -- Nevertheless, to avoid fornication, let every man have his own wife, and let every woman have her own husband.

1 Corinthians 7:4-5 -- The wife hath not power of her own body, but the husband: and likewise also the husband hath not power of his own body, but the wife. Defraud ye not one the other, except it be with consent for a time, that ye may give yourselves to fasting and prayer; and come together again, that Satan tempt you not for your incontinency.

1 Corinthians 7:14 -- For the unbelieving husband is sanctified by the wife, and the unbelieving wife is sanctified by the husband: else were your children unclean; but now are they holy.

1 Corinthians 7:33 -- But he that is married careth for the things that are of the world, how he may please his wife.

1 Peter 3:1 -- Likewise, ye wives, be in subjection to your own husbands; that, if any obey not the word, they also may without the word be won by the conversation of the wives;

Ecclesiastes 9:9 -- Live joyfully with the wife whom thou lovest all the days of the life of thy vanity, which he hath given thee under the sun, all the days of thy vanity: for that is thy portion in this life, and in thy labour which thou takest under the sun.

Ephesians 5:22-23 -- Wives, submit yourselves unto your own husbands, as unto the Lord. For the husband is the head of the wife, even as Christ is the head of the church: and he is the saviour of the body.

Ephesians 5:25-29 -- Husbands, love your wives, even as Christ also loved the church, and gave himself for it; That he might sanctify and cleanse it with the washing of water by the word, hat he might present it to himself a glorious church, not having spot, or wrinkle, or any such thing; but that it should be holy and without blemish. So ought men to love their wives as their own bodies. He that loveth his wife loveth himself. For no man ever yet hated his own flesh; but nourisheth and cherisheth it, even as the Lord the church:

Proverbs 5:15 -- Drink waters out of thine own cistern, and running waters out of thine own well.

Proverbs 11:16 -- A gracious woman retaineth honour: and strong men retain riches.

Proverbs 12:4 -- A virtuous woman is a crown to her husband: but she that maketh ashamed is as rottenness in his bones.

Proverbs 18:22 -- Whoso findeth a wife findeth a good thing, and obtaineth favour of the LORD.

Proverbs 19:14 -- House and riches are the inheritance of fathers: and a prudent wife is from the LORD.

Proverbs 19:20 -- Hear counsel, and receive instruction, that thou mayest be wise in thy latter end.

Proverbs 31:10 -- Who can find a virtuous woman? for her price is far above rubies.

Proverbs 31:23 -- Her husband is known in the gates, when he sitteth among the elders of the land.

Proverbs 31:30 -- Favour is deceitful, and beauty is vain: but a woman that feareth the LORD, she shall be praised.

Psalm 128:3 -- Thy wife shall be as a fruitful vine by the sides of thine house: thy children like olive plants round about thy table.

Titus 2:3-4 -- The aged women likewise, that they be in behaviour as becometh holiness, not false accusers, not given to much wine, teachers of good things; That they may teach the young women to be sober, to love their husbands, to love their children,

Singleness
2 Corinthians 6:18 -- *And will be a Father unto you, and ye shall be my sons and daughters, saith the Lord Almighty.*

1 Corinthians 10:13 -- There hath no temptation taken you but such as is common to man: but God is faithful, who will not suffer you to be tempted above that ye are able; but will with the temptation also make a way to escape, that ye may be able to bear it.

1 Corinthians 6:15 -- Know ye not that your bodies are the members of Christ? shall I then take the members of Christ, and make them the members of an harlot? God forbid.

1 Peter 1:6 -- Wherein ye greatly rejoice, though now for a season, if need be, ye are in heaviness through manifold temptations:

1 Peter 2:11 -- Dearly beloved, I beseech you as strangers and

pilgrims, abstain from fleshly lusts, which war against the soul;

1 Thessalonians 4:3-4 -- For this is the will of God, even your sanctification, that ye should abstain from fornication: That every one of you should know how to possess his vessel in sanctification and honour;

2 Corinthians 6:14 -- Be ye not unequally yoked together with unbelievers: for what fellowship hath righteousness with unrighteousness? and what communion hath light with darkness?

2 Peter 2:9 -- The Lord knoweth how to deliver the godly out of temptations, and to reserve the unjust unto the day of judgment to be punished:

Hebrews 13:5 -- Let your conversation be without covetousness; and be content with such things as ye have: for he hath said, I will never leave thee, nor forsake thee.

Proverbs 18:22 -- Whoso findeth a wife findeth a good thing, and obtaineth favour of the LORD.

John 10:27 -- My sheep hear my voice, and I know them, and they follow me:

Joshua 1:5 -- There shall not any man be able to stand before thee all the days of thy life: as I was with Moses, so I will be with thee: I will not fail thee, nor forsake thee.

Matthew 18:20 -- For where two or three are gathered together in my name, there am I in the midst of them.

Proverbs 17:17 -- A friend loveth at all times, and a brother is born for adversity.

Proverbs 18:24 -- A man that hath friends must shew himself friendly: and there is a friend that sticketh closer than a brother.

James 1:2-3 -- My brethren, count it all joy when ye fall into divers temptations; Knowing this, that the trying of your faith worketh patience.

James 1:13 -- Let no man say when he is tempted, I am tempted of God: for God cannot be tempted with evil, neither tempteth he any man:

James 1:4 -- But let patience have her perfect work, that ye may be perfect and entire, wanting nothing.

Matthew 26:41 -- Watch and pray, that ye enter not into temptation: the spirit indeed is willing, but the flesh is weak.

Proverbs 1:10 -- My son, if sinners entice thee, consent thou not.

Proverbs 2:11 -- Discretion shall preserve thee, understanding shall keep thee:

Proverbs 4:14 -- Enter not into the path of the wicked, and go not in the way of evil men.

Revelations 3:10 -- Because thou hast kept the word of my patience, I also will keep thee from the hour of temptation, which shall come upon all the world, to try them that dwell upon the earth.

Families

Deuteronomy 12:7 -- *And there ye shall eat before the LORD your God, and ye shall rejoice in all that ye put your hand unto, ye and your households, wherein the LORD thy God hath blessed thee.*

1 Timothy 3:12 -- Let the deacons be the husbands of one wife, ruling their children and their own houses well.

Acts 16:31 -- And they said, Believe on the Lord Jesus Christ, and thou shalt be saved, and thy house.

Deuteronomy 11:19 -- And ye shall teach them your children, speaking of them when thou sittest in thine house, and when thou walkest by the way, when thou liest down, and when thou risest up.

Ephesians 2:19 -- Now therefore ye are no more strangers and foreigners, but fellow citizens with the saints, and of the household of God;

Genesis 12:3 -- And I will bless them that bless thee, and curse him that curseth thee: and in thee shall all families of the earth be blessed.

Proverbs 4:5 -- Get wisdom, get understanding: forget it not; neither decline from the words of my mouth.

Proverbs 4:10 -- Hear, O my son, and receive my sayings; and the years of thy life shall be many.

Proverbs 8:33 -- Hear instruction, and be wise, and refuse it not.

Proverbs 20:7 -- The just man walketh in his integrity: his children are blessed after him.

Proverbs 22:6 -- Train up a child in the way he should go: and when he is old, he will not depart from it.

Psalm 68:6 -- God setteth the solitary in families: he bringeth out those which are bound with chains: but the rebellious dwell in a dry land.

Psalm 103:13 -- Like as a father pitieth his children, so the LORD pitieth them that fear him.

Psalm 113:9 -- He maketh the barren woman to keep house, and to be a joyful mother of children. Praise ye the LORD.

Psalm 127:2-5 -- It is vain for you to rise up early, to sit up late, to eat the bread of sorrows: for so he giveth his beloved sleep. Lo, children are an heritage of the LORD: and the fruit of the womb is his reward. As arrows are in the hand of a mighty man; so are children of the youth. Happy is the man that hath his quiver full of them: they shall not be ashamed, but they shall speak with the enemies in the gate.

Psalm 128:3-4 -- Thy wife shall be as a fruitful vine by the sides of thine house: thy children like olive plants round about thy table. Behold, that thus shall the man be blessed that feareth the LORD.

Psalm 128:6 -- Yea, thou shalt see thy children's children, and peace upon Israel.

Children
Proverbs 22:6 -- Train up a child in the way he should go: and when he is old, he will not depart from it.

Ephesians 6:1-3 -- Children, obey your parents in the Lord: for this is right. Honour thy father and mother; (which is the first commandment with promise;) That it may be well with thee, and thou mayest live long on the earth.

Isaiah 54:13 -- And all thy children shall be taught of the LORD; and great shall be the peace of thy children.

Jeremiah 1:5-7 -- Before I formed thee in the belly I knew thee; and before thou camest forth out of the womb I sanctified thee, and I ordained thee a prophet unto the nations. Then said I, Ah, Lord GOD! behold, I cannot speak: for I am a child. But the LORD said unto me, Say not, I am a child: for thou shalt go to all that I shall send thee, and whatsoever I command thee thou shalt speak.

Jeremiah 1:10 -- See, I have this day set thee over the nations and over the kingdoms, to root out, and to pull down, and to destroy, and to throw down, to build, and to plant.

John 14:6 -- Jesus saith unto him, I am the way, the truth, and the life: no man cometh unto the Father, but by me.

Proverbs 3:1-2 -- My son, forget not my law; but let thine heart keep my commandments: For length of days, and long life, and peace, shall they add to thee.

Proverbs 8:6-7 -- Hear; for I will speak of excellent things; and the opening of my lips shall be right things. For my mouth shall speak truth; and wickedness is an abomination to my lips.

Proverbs 13:1 -- A wise son heareth his father's instruction: but a scorner heareth not rebuke.

Proverbs 15:31 -- The ear that heareth the reproof of life abideth among the wise.

Proverbs 17:6 -- Children's children are the crown of old men; and the glory of children are their fathers.

Proverbs 20:7 -- The just man walketh in his integrity: his children are blessed after him.

Proverbs 20:11 -- Even a child is known by his doings, whether his work be pure, and whether it be right.

Psalm 37:4 -- Delight thyself also in the LORD; and he shall give thee the desires of thine heart.

Psalm 78:6 -- That the generation to come might know them, even the children which should be born; who should arise and declare them to their children:

Psalm 115:16 -- The heaven, even the heavens, are the LORD'S: but the earth hath he given to the children of men.

Psalm 128:3 -- Thy wife shall be as a fruitful vine by the sides of thine house: thy children like olive plants round about thy table.

Orphans / Children of Singles / Widows
Deuteronomy 10:18 -- *He doth execute the judgment of the fatherless and widow, and loveth the stranger, in giving him food and raiment.*

Deuteronomy 27:19 -- Cursed be he that perverteth the judgment of the stranger, fatherless, and widow. And all the people shall say, Amen.

Job 29:12 -- Because I delivered the poor that cried, and the fatherless, and him that had none to help him.

Malachi 3:5 -- And I will come near to you to judgment; and I will be a swift witness against the sorcerers, and against the adulterers, and against false swearers, and against those that oppress the hireling in his wages, the widow, and the fatherless, and that turn aside the stranger from his right, and fear not me, saith the LORD of hosts.

Proverb 31:9 -- Open thy mouth, judge righteously, and plead the cause of the poor and needy.

Psalm 10:14 -- Thou hast seen it; for thou beholdest mischief and spite, to requite it with thy hand: the poor committeth himself unto thee; thou art the helper of the fatherless.

Psalm 10:18 -- To judge the fatherless and the oppressed, that the man of the earth may no more oppress.

Psalm 146:9 -- The LORD preserveth the strangers; he relieveth the fatherless and widow: but the way of the wicked he turneth upside down.

FINANCES

Finances

Matthew 6:33 -- *But seek ye first the kingdom of God,
and his righteousness; and all these things
shall be added unto you.*

1 Kings 17:15-16 -- And she went and did according to the saying of Elijah: and she, and he, and her house, did eat many days. And the barrel of meal wasted not, neither did the cruse of oil fail, according to the word of the LORD, which he spake by Elijah.

2 Corinthians 9:7 -- Every man according as he purposeth in his heart, so let him give; not grudgingly, or of necessity: for God loveth a cheerful giver.

2 Peter 1:3 -- According as his divine power hath given unto us all things that pertain unto life and godliness, through the knowledge of him that hath called us to glory and virtue:

3 John 1:2 -- Beloved, I wish above all things that thou mayest prosper and be in health, even as thy soul prospereth.

Deuteronomy 16:17 -- Every man shall give as he is able, according to the blessing of the LORD thy God which he hath given thee.

Deuteronomy 28:1-2 -- And it shall come to pass, if thou shalt hearken diligently unto the voice of the LORD thy God, to observe and to do all his commandments which I command thee this day, that the LORD thy God will set thee on high above all nations of the earth: And all these blessings shall come on thee, and overtake thee, if thou shalt hearken unto the voice of the LORD thy God.

Deuteronomy 8:18 -- But thou shalt remember the LORD thy God: for it is he that giveth thee power to get wealth, that he may establish his covenant which he sware unto thy fathers, as it is this day.

Ephesians 3:20 -- Now unto him that is able to do exceeding abundantly above all that we ask or think, according to the power that worketh in us,

Galatians 6:7 -- Be not deceived; God is not mocked: for whatsoever a man soweth, that shall he also reap.

Galatians 6:9 -- And let us not be weary in well doing: for in due season we shall reap, if we faint not.

Isaiah 1:19 -- If ye be willing and obedient, ye shall eat the good of the land:

Joshua 1:8 -- This book of the law shall not depart out of thy mouth; but thou shalt meditate therein day and night, that thou mayest observe to do according to all that is written therein: for then thou shalt make thy way prosperous, and then thou shalt have good success.

Luke 12:32 -- Fear not, little flock; for it is your Father's good pleasure to give you the kingdom.

Luke 12:34 -- For where your treasure is, there will your heart be also.

Luke 12:44 -- Of a truth I say unto you, that he will make him ruler over all that he hath.

Luke 16:11 -- If therefore ye have not been faithful in the unrighteous mammon, who will commit to your trust the true riches?

Luke 6:38 -- Give, and it shall be given unto you; good measure, pressed down, and shaken together, and running over, shall men give into your bosom. For with the same measure that ye mete withal it shall be measured to you again.

Malachi 3:10 -- Bring ye all the tithes into the storehouse, that there may be meat in mine house, and prove me now herewith, saith the LORD of hosts, if I will not open you the windows of heaven, and pour you out a blessing, that there shall not be room enough to receive it.

Proverbs 10:22 -- The blessing of the LORD, it maketh rich, and he addeth no sorrow with it.

Proverbs 13:22 -- A good man leaveth an inheritance to his children's children: and the wealth of the sinner is laid up for the just.

Proverbs 24:3-4 -- Through wisdom is an house builded; and by understanding it is established: And by knowledge shall the chambers be filled with all precious and pleasant riches.

Proverbs 3:9-10 -- Honour the LORD with thy substance, and with the firstfruits of all thine increase: So shall thy barns be filled with plenty, and thy presses shall burst out with new wine.

Psalm 34:10 -- The young lions do lack, and suffer hunger: but they that seek the LORD shall not want any good thing.

Psalm 35:27 -- Let them shout for joy, and be glad, that favour my righteous cause: yea, let them say continually, Let the LORD be magnified, which hath pleasure in the prosperity of his servant.

Psalm 37:25 -- I have been young, and now am old; yet have I not seen the righteous forsaken, nor his seed begging bread.

Psalm 50:14 -- Offer unto God thanksgiving; and pay thy vows unto the most High:

Psalm 66:12 -- Thou hast caused men to ride over our heads; we went through fire and through water: but thou broughtest us out into a wealthy place.

Psalm 68:19 -- Blessed be the Lord, who daily loadeth us with benefits, even the God of our salvation. Selah.

Psalm 84:11 -- For the LORD God is a sun and shield: the LORD will give grace and glory: no good thing will he withhold from them that walk uprightly.

Psalm 112:1-3 -- Praise ye the LORD. Blessed is the man that feareth the LORD, that delighteth greatly in his commandments. His seed shall be mighty upon earth: the generation of the upright shall be blessed. Wealth and riches shall be in his house: and his righteousness endureth for ever.

Psalm 112:5 -- A good man sheweth favour, and lendeth: he will guide his affairs with discretion.

Romans 13:8 -- Owe no man any thing, but to love one another: for he that loveth another hath fulfilled the law.

Abundance & Increase
Matthew 6:33 -- *But seek ye first the kingdom of God, and his righteousness; and all these things shall be added unto you.*

3 John 1:2 -- Beloved, I wish above all things that thou mayest prosper and be in health, even as thy soul prospereth.

Colossians 1:10 -- That ye might walk worthy of the Lord unto all pleasing, being fruitful in every good work, and increasing in the knowledge of God;

Ephesians 3:20 -- Now unto him that is able to do exceeding abundantly above all that we ask or think, according to the power that worketh in us,

Genesis 15:1 -- After these things the word of the LORD came unto Abram in a vision, saying, Fear not, Abram: I am thy shield, and thy exceeding great reward.

Isaiah 29:19 -- The meek also shall increase their joy in the LORD, and the poor among men shall rejoice in the Holy One of Israel.

Jeremiah 31:14 -- And I will satiate the soul of the priests with fatness, and my people shall be satisfied with my goodness, saith the LORD.

Job 8:7 -- Though thy beginning was small, yet thy latter end should greatly increase.

Leviticus 26:4 -- Then I will give you rain in due season, and the land shall yield her increase, and the trees of the field shall yield their fruit

Malachi 3:11-12 -- And I will rebuke the devourer for your sakes, and he shall not destroy the fruits of your ground; neither shall your vine cast her fruit before the time in the field, saith the LORD of hosts. And all nations shall call you blessed: for ye shall be a delightsome land, saith the LORD of hosts.

Philippians 4:19 -- But my God shall supply all your need according to his riches in glory by Christ Jesus.

Proverbs 10:22 -- The blessing of the LORD, it maketh rich, and he addeth no sorrow with it.

Proverbs 11:25 -- The liberal soul shall be made fat: and he that watereth shall be watered also himself.

Proverbs 15:16 -- Better is little with the fear of the LORD than great treasure and trouble therewith.

Proverbs 16:7 -- When a man's ways please the LORD, he maketh even his enemies to be at peace with him.

Proverbs 22:1 -- A good name is rather to be chosen than great riches, and loving favour rather than silver and gold.

Proverbs 22:16 -- He that oppresseth the poor to increase his riches, and he that giveth to the rich, shall surely come to want.

Proverbs 3:9-10 -- Honour the LORD with thy substance, and with the firstfruits of all thine increase: So shall thy barns be filled with plenty, and thy presses shall burst out with new wine.

Proverbs 9:9 -- Give instruction to a wise man, and he will be yet wiser: teach a just man, and he will increase in learning.

Psalm 62:10 -- Trust not in oppression, and become not vain in robbery: if riches increase, set not your heart upon them.

Psalm 85:12 -- Yea, the LORD shall give that which is good; and our land shall yield her increase.

Blessings

Exodus 23:25 -- And ye shall serve the LORD your God, and he shall bless thy bread, and thy water; and I will take sickness away from the midst of thee.

Deuteronomy 28:8 -- The LORD shall command the blessing upon thee in thy storehouses, and in all that thou settest thine hand unto; and he shall bless thee in the land which the LORD thy God giveth thee.

Genesis 12:3 -- And I will bless them that bless thee, and curse him that curseth thee: and in thee shall all families of the earth be blessed.

Genesis 22:17-18 -- That in blessing I will bless thee, and in multiplying I will multiply thy seed as the stars of the heaven, and as the sand which is upon the sea shore; and thy seed shall possess the gate of his enemies; And in thy seed shall all the nations of the earth be blessed; because thou hast obeyed my voice.

Genesis 28:3 -- And God Almighty bless thee, and make thee fruitful, and multiply thee, that thou mayest be a multitude of people;

Isaiah 44:3 -- For I will pour water upon him that is thirsty, and floods upon the dry ground: I will pour my spirit upon thy seed, and my blessing upon thine offspring:

Numbers 6:24-25 -- The LORD bless thee, and keep thee: The LORD make his face shine upon thee, and be gracious unto thee:

Proverbs 11:11 -- By the blessing of the upright the city is exalted: but it is overthrown by the mouth of the wicked.

Proverbs 20:7 -- The just man walketh in his integrity: his children are blessed after him.

Proverbs 8:32 -- Now therefore hearken unto me, O ye children: for blessed are they that keep my ways.

Psalm 5:12 -- For thou, LORD, wilt bless the righteous; with favour wilt thou compass him as with a shield.

Psalm 84:5 -- Blessed is the man whose strength is in thee; in whose heart are the ways of them.

Psalm 89:15 -- Blessed is the people that know the joyful sound: they shall walk, O LORD, in the light of thy countenance.

Prosperity

Psalm 35:27 -- Let them shout for joy, and be glad, that favour my righteous cause: yea, let them say continually, Let the LORD be magnified, which hath pleasure in the prosperity of his servant.

1 Corinthians 16:2 -- Upon the first day of the week let every one of you lay by him in store, as God hath prospered him, that there be no gatherings when I come.

Joshua 1:7 -- Only be thou strong and very courageous, that thou mayest observe to do according to all the law, which Moses my servant commanded thee: turn not from it to the right hand or to the left, that thou mayest prosper whithersoever thou goest.

Nehemiah 1:11 -- O Lord, I beseech thee, let now thine ear be attentive to the prayer of thy servant, and to the prayer of thy servants, who desire to fear thy name: and prosper, I pray thee, thy servant this day, and grant him mercy in the sight of this man. For I was the king's cupbearer.

Psalm 118:25 -- Save now, I beseech thee, O LORD: O LORD, I beseech thee, send now prosperity.

Psalm 122:7 -- Peace be within thy walls, and prosperity within thy palaces.

Zechariah 8:12 -- For the seed shall be prosperous; the vine shall give her fruit, and the ground shall give her increase, and the heavens shall give their dew; and I will cause the remnant of this people to possess all these things.

Direction
Isaiah 42:16 -- *And I will bring the blind by a way that they knew not; I will lead them in paths that they have not known: I will make darkness light before them, and crooked things straight. These things will I do unto them, and not forsake them.*

Guidance
Psalm 32:8 -- *I will instruct thee and teach thee in the way which thou shalt go: I will guide thee with mine eye.*

Ephesians 1:11 -- In whom also we have obtained an inheritance, being predestinated according to the purpose of him who worketh all things after the counsel of his own will:

Exodus 15:13 -- Thou in thy mercy hast led forth the people which thou hast redeemed: thou hast guided them in thy strength unto thy holy habitation.

Isaiah 58:11 -- And the LORD shall guide thee continually, and satisfy thy soul in drought, and make fat thy bones: and thou shalt be like a watered garden, and like a spring of water, whose waters fail not.

Jeremiah 33:3 -- Call unto me, and I will answer thee, and shew thee great and mighty things, which thou knowest not.

Job 32:8 -- But there is a spirit in man: and the inspiration of the Almighty giveth them understanding.

John 16:13 -- Howbeit when he, the Spirit of truth, is come, he will guide you into all truth: for he shall not speak of himself; but whatsoever he shall hear, that shall he speak: and he will shew you things to come.

Luke 1:79 -- To give light to them that sit in darkness and in the shadow of death, to guide our feet into the way of peace.

Micah 7:5 -- Trust ye not in a friend, put ye not confidence in a guide: keep the doors of thy mouth from her that lieth in thy bosom.

Proverbs 16:23 -- The heart of the wise teacheth his mouth, and addeth learning to his lips.

Proverbs 16:3 -- Commit thy works unto the LORD, and thy thoughts shall be established.

Proverbs 16:9 -- A man's heart deviseth his way: but the LORD directeth his steps.

Proverbs 24:3-24 -- Through wisdom is an house builded; and by understanding it is established: And by knowledge shall the chambers be filled with all precious and pleasant riches.

Psalm 16:11 -- Thou wilt shew me the path of life: in thy presence is fulness of joy; at thy right hand there are pleasures for evermore.

Psalm 16:7 -- I will bless the LORD, who hath given me counsel: my reins also instruct me in the night seasons.

Psalm 25:4 -- Shew me thy ways, O LORD; teach me thy paths.

Psalm 25:9 -- The meek will he guide in judgment: and the meek will he teach his way.

Psalm 27:13-14 -- I had fainted, unless I had believed to see the goodness of the LORD in the land of the living. Wait on the LORD: be of good courage, and he shall strengthen thine heart: wait, I say, on the LORD.

Psalm 31:3 -- For thou art my rock and my fortress; therefore for thy name's sake lead me, and guide me.

Psalm 32:8 -- I will instruct thee and teach thee in the way which thou shalt go: I will guide thee with mine eye.

Psalm 43:3 -- O send out thy light and thy truth: let them lead me; let them bring me unto thy holy hill, and to thy tabernacles.

Psalm 5:8 -- Lead me, O LORD, in thy righteousness because of mine enemies; make thy way straight before my face.

Psalm 73:24 -- Thou shalt guide me with thy counsel, and afterward receive me to glory.

Psalm 78:72 -- So he fed them according to the integrity of his heart; and guided them by the skillfulness of his hands.

Psalm 112:5 -- A good man sheweth favour, and lendeth: he will guide his affairs with discretion.

Psalm 119:133 -- Order my steps in thy word: and let not any iniquity have dominion over me.

Revelations 7:17 -- For the Lamb which is in the midst of the throne shall feed them, and shall lead them unto living fountains of waters: and God shall wipe away all tears from their eyes.

Romans 8:14 -- For as many as are led by the Spirit of God, they are the sons of God.

Making Decisions

Jeremiah 33:3 -- *Call unto me, and I will answer thee, and shew thee great and mighty things, which thou knowest not.*

1 Corinthians 4:5 -- Therefore judge nothing before the time, until the Lord come, who both will bring to light the hidden things of darkness, and will make manifest the counsels of the hearts: and then shall every man have praise of God.

1 John 2:20 -- But ye have an unction from the Holy One, and ye know all things.

1 Peter 5:10 -- But the God of all grace, who hath called us unto his eternal glory by Christ Jesus, after that ye have suffered a while, make you perfect, stablish, strengthen, settle you.

Colossians 1:9 -- For this cause we also, since the day we heard it, do not cease to pray for you, and to desire that ye might be filled with the knowledge of his will in all wisdom and spiritual understanding;

Ephesians 1:11 -- In whom also we have obtained an inheritance, being predestinated according to the purpose of him who worketh all things after the counsel of his own will:

Ephesians 1:17-19 -- That the God of our Lord Jesus Christ, the Father of glory, may give unto you the spirit of wisdom and revelation in the knowledge of him: The eyes of your understanding being enlightened; that ye may know what is the hope of his calling, and what the riches of the glory of his inheritance in the saints, And what is the exceeding greatness of his power to us-ward who believe, according to the working of his mighty power,

Ephesians 5:17 -- Wherefore be ye not unwise, but understanding what the will of the Lord is.

Hebrews 6:17 -- Wherein God, willing more abundantly to shew unto the heirs of promise the immutability of his counsel, confirmed it by an oath:

Isaiah 30:21 -- And thine ears shall hear a word behind thee, saying, This is the way, walk ye in it, when ye turn to the right hand, and when ye turn to the left.

Luke 24:45 -- Then opened he their understanding, that they might understand the scriptures,

Proverbs 1:23 -- Turn you at my reproof: behold, I will pour out my spirit unto you, I will make known my words unto you.

Proverbs 24:6 -- For by wise counsel thou shalt make thy war: and in multitude of counsellors there is safety.

Proverbs 3:13 -- Happy is the man that findeth wisdom, and the man that getteth understanding.

Proverbs 3:5-6 -- Trust in the LORD with all thine heart; and lean not unto thine own understanding. In all thy ways acknowledge him, and he shall direct thy paths.

Proverbs 8:14 -- Counsel is mine, and sound wisdom: I am understanding; I have strength.

Psalm 18:30 -- As for God, his way is perfect: the word of the LORD is tried: he is a buckler to all those that trust in him.

Psalm 32:8 -- I will instruct thee and teach thee in the way which thou shalt go: I will guide thee with mine eye.

Psalm 119:125 -- I am thy servant; give me understanding, that I may know thy testimonies.

Psalm 119:130 -- The entrance of thy words giveth light; it giveth understanding unto the simple.

Psalm 119:169 -- Let my cry come near before thee, O LORD: give me understanding according to thy word.

Possessing Property

Exd 22:7 -- *If a man shall deliver unto his neighbour money or stuff to keep, and it be stolen out of the man's house; if the thief be found, let him pay double.*

Deuteronomy 1:21 -- Behold, the LORD thy God hath set the land before thee: go up and possess it, as the LORD God of thy fathers hath said unto thee; fear not, neither be discouraged.

Ezekiel 28:26 -- And they shall dwell safely therein, and shall build houses, and plant vineyards; yea, they shall dwell with confidence, when I have executed judgments upon all those that despise them round about them; and they shall know that I am the LORD their God.

Jeremiah 29:5 -- Build ye houses, and dwell in them; and plant gardens, and eat the fruit of them;

Job 21:9 -- Their houses are safe from fear, neither is the rod of God upon them.

Nehemiah 9:25 -- And they took strong cities, and a fat land, and possessed houses full of all goods, wells digged, vineyards, and oliveyards, and fruit trees in abundance: so they did eat, and were filled, and became fat, and delighted themselves in thy great goodness.

Overcoming Indebtedness

Malachi 3:10 -- *Bring ye all the tithes into the storehouse, that there may be meat in mine house, and prove me now herewith, saith the LORD of hosts, if I will not open you the windows of heaven, and pour you out a blessing, that there shall not be room enough to receive it.*

Ephesians 6:8 -- Knowing that whatsoever good thing any man doeth, the same shall he receive of the Lord, whether he be bond or free.

Mark 11:23 -- For verily I say unto you, That whosoever shall say unto this mountain, Be thou removed, and be thou cast into the sea; and shall not doubt in his heart, but shall believe that those things which he saith shall come to pass; he shall have whatsoever he saith.

Matthew 12:29 -- Or else how can one enter into a strong man's house, and spoil his goods, except he first bind the strong man? and then he will spoil his house.

Matthew 6:12 -- And forgive us our debts, as we forgive our debtors.

Proverbs 13:22 -- A good man leaveth an inheritance to his children's children: and the wealth of the sinner is laid up for the just.

Romans 13:8 -- Owe no man any thing, but to love one another: for he that loveth another hath fulfilled the law.

CAREER

Career Decision
Isaiah 48:17 -- *Thus saith the LORD, thy Redeemer, the Holy One of Israel; I am the LORD thy God which teacheth thee to profit, which leadeth thee by the way that thou shouldest go.*

2 Corinthians 9:8 -- And God is able to make all grace abound toward you; that ye, always having all sufficiency in all things, may abound to every good work:

Hebrews 10:35 -- Cast not away therefore your confidence, which hath great recompence of reward.

Isaiah 30:21 -- And thine ears shall hear a word behind thee, saying, This is the way, walk ye in it, when ye turn to the right hand, and when ye turn to the left.

Isaiah 42:16 -- And I will bring the blind by a way that they knew not; I will lead them in paths that they have not known: I will make darkness light before them, and crooked things straight. These things will I do unto them, and not forsake them.

Jeremiah 17:7 -- Blessed is the man that trusteth in the LORD, and whose hope the LORD is.

Joshua 1:8 -- This book of the law shall not depart out of thy mouth; but thou shalt meditate therein day and night, that thou mayest observe to do according to all that is written therein: for then thou shalt make thy way prosperous, and then thou shalt have good success.

Mark 9:23 -- Jesus said unto him, If thou canst believe, all things are possible to him that believeth.

Matthew 6:8 -- Be not ye therefore like unto them: for your Father knoweth what things ye have need of, before ye ask him.

Matthew 6:26 -- Behold the fowls of the air: for they sow not, neither do they reap, nor gather into barns; yet your heavenly Father feedeth them. Are ye not much better than they?

Philippians 4:6 -- Be careful for nothing; but in every thing by prayer and supplication with thanksgiving let your requests be made known unto God.

Proverbs 20:5 -- Counsel in the heart of man is like deep water; but a man of understanding will draw it out.

Proverbs 29:25 -- The fear of man bringeth a snare: but whoso putteth his trust in the LORD shall be safe.

Psalm 32:8 -- I will instruct thee and teach thee in the way which thou shalt go: I will guide thee with mine eye.

Psalm 90:12 -- So teach us to number our days, that we may apply our hearts unto wisdom.

Jeremiah 17:7 -- Blessed is the man that trusteth in the LORD, and whose hope the LORD is.

Employment

1 Timothy 5:8 -- But if any provide not for his own, and specially for those of his own house, he hath denied the faith, and is worse than an infidel.

1 Corinthians 9:10 -- Or saith he it altogether for our sakes? For our sakes, no doubt, this is written: that he that ploweth should plow in hope; and that he that thresheth in hope should be partaker of his hope.

2 Timothy 2:15 -- Study to shew thyself approved unto God, a workman that needeth not to be ashamed, rightly dividing the word of truth.

Colossians 1:10 -- That ye might walk worthy of the Lord unto all pleasing, being fruitful in every good work, and increasing in the knowledge of God;

Deuteronomy 2:7 -- For the LORD thy God hath blessed thee in all the works of thy hand: he knoweth thy walking through this great wilderness: these forty years the LORD thy God hath been with thee; thou hast lacked nothing.

Habakkuk 1:5 -- Behold ye among the heathen, and regard, and wonder marvellously: for I will work a work in your days, which ye will not believe, though it be told you.

John 6:28 -- Then said they unto him, What shall we do, that we might work the works of God?

Matthew 11:28 -- Come unto me, all ye that labour and are heavy laden, and I will give you rest.

Zechariah 4:6 -- Then he answered and spake unto me, saying, This is the word of the LORD unto Zerubbabel, saying, Not by might, nor by power, but by my spirit, saith the LORD of hosts.

Faithful in Service & Stewardship
Colossians 3:22 -- *Servants, obey in all things your masters according to the flesh; not with eyeservice, as menpleasers; but in singleness of heart, fearing God:*

1 Corinthians 4:2 -- Moreover it is required in stewards, that a man be found faithful.

1 Peter 2:18 -- Servants, be subject to your masters with all fear; not only to the good and gentle, but also to the froward.

1 Timothy 6:1-2 -- Let as many servants as are under the yoke count their own masters worthy of all honour, that the name of God and his doctrine be not blasphemed. And they that have believing masters, let them not despise them, because they are brethren; but rather do them service, because they are faithful and beloved, partakers of the benefit. These things teach and exhort.

Colossians 3:23-24 -- And whatsoever ye do, do it heartily, as to the Lord, and not unto men; Knowing that of the Lord ye shall receive the reward of the inheritance: for ye serve the Lord Christ.

Ephesians 6:6-8 -- Not with eyeservice, as menpleasers; but as the servants of Christ, doing the will of God from the heart; With good will doing service, as to the Lord, and not to men: Knowing that whatsoever good thing any man doeth, the same shall he receive of the Lord, whether he be bond or free.

Jeremiah 22:13 -- Woe unto him that buildeth his house by unrighteousness, and his chambers by wrong; that useth his neighbour's service without wages, and giveth him not for his work;

John 13:16 -- Verily, verily, I say unto you, The servant is not greater than his lord; neither he that is sent greater than he that sent him.

Leviticus 19:13 -- Thou shalt not defraud thy neighbour, neither rob him: the wages of him that is hired shall not abide with thee all night until the morning.

Luke 12:37 -- Blessed are those servants, whom the lord when he cometh shall find watching: verily I say unto you, that he shall gird himself, and make them to sit down to meat, and will come forth and serve them.

Luke 16:10 -- He that is faithful in that which is least is faithful also in much: and he that is unjust in the least is unjust also in much.

Luke 16:12 -- And if ye have not been faithful in that which is another man's, who shall give you that which is your own?

Matthew 24:45 -- Who then is a faithful and wise servant, whom his lord hath made ruler over his household, to give them meat in due season?

Matthew 24:46-47 -- Blessed is that servant, whom his lord when he cometh shall find so doing. Verily I say unto you, That he shall make him ruler over all his goods.

Titus 2:9 -- Exhort servants to be obedient unto their own masters, and to please them well in all things; not answering again;

Career Success

Colossians 3:23 -- And whatsoever ye do, do it heartily, as to the Lord, and not unto men;

1 Kings 6:14 -- So Solomon built the house, and finished it.

2 Timothy 4:7 -- I have fought a good fight, I have finished my course, I have kept the faith:

Acts 20:24 -- But none of these things move me, neither count I my life dear unto myself, so that I might finish my course with joy, and the ministry, which I have received of the Lord Jesus, to testify the gospel of the grace of God.

Colossians 3:17 -- And whatsoever ye do in word or deed, do all in the name of the Lord Jesus, giving thanks to God and the Father by him.

Galatians 6:9 -- And let us not be weary in well doing: for in due season we shall reap, if we faint not.

Romans 9:28 -- For he will finish the work, and cut it short in righteousness: because a short work will the Lord make upon the earth.

Working Senior

Job 12:12-13 -- With the ancient is wisdom; and in length of days understanding. With him is wisdom and strength, he hath counsel and understanding.

Deuteronomy 5:33 -- Ye shall walk in all the ways which the LORD your God hath commanded you, that ye may live, and that it may be well with you, and that ye may prolong your days in the land which ye shall possess.

Isaiah 46:4 -- And even to your old age I am he; and even to hoar hairs will I carry you: I have made, and I will bear; even I will carry, and will deliver you.

Job 11:17 -- And thine age shall be clearer than the noonday; thou shalt shine forth, thou shalt be as the morning.

Proverbs 3:1 -- My son, forget not my law; but let thine heart keep my commandments:

Proverbs 3:2 -- For length of days, and long life, and peace, shall they add to thee.

Proverbs 9:11 -- For by me thy days shall be multiplied, and the years of thy life shall be increased.

Proverbs 10:27 -- The fear of the LORD prolongeth days: but the years of the wicked shall be shortened.

Proverbs 20:29 -- The glory of young men is their strength: and the beauty of old men is the gray head.

Psalm 39:4 -- LORD, make me to know mine end, and the measure of my days, what it is; that I may know how frail I am.

Psalm 91:16 -- With long life will I satisfy him, and shew him my salvation.

Titus 2:1-3 -- But speak thou the things which become sound doctrine: That the aged men be sober, grave, temperate, sound in faith, in charity, in patience. The aged women likewise, that they be in behaviour as becometh holiness, not false accusers, not given to much wine, teachers of good things;

STUDENTS

Students
Proverbs 16:23 -- *The heart of the wise teacheth his mouth, and addeth learning to his lips.*

1 Thessalonians 4:11 -- And that ye study to be quiet, and to do your own business, and to work with your own hands, as we commanded you;
2 Timothy 2:15 -- Study to shew thyself approved unto God, a workman that needeth not to be ashamed, rightly dividing the word of truth.
2 Timothy 3:14 -- But continue thou in the things which thou hast learned and hast been assured of, knowing of whom thou hast learned them;
Isaiah 50:4 -- The Lord GOD hath given me the tongue of the learned, that I should know how to speak a word in season to him that is weary: he wakeneth morning by morning, he wakeneth mine ear to hear as the learned.
Proverbs 1:5 -- A wise man will hear, and will increase learning; and a man of understanding shall attain unto wise counsels:
Proverbs 2:10-11 -- When wisdom entereth into thine heart, and knowledge is pleasant unto thy soul; Discretion shall preserve thee, understanding shall keep thee:
Proverbs 16:21 -- The wise in heart shall be called prudent: and the sweetness of the lips increaseth learning.
Psalm 32:8 -- I will instruct thee and teach thee in the way which thou shalt go: I will guide thee with mine eye.

Focus / Concentration
Philippians 4:8 -- *Finally, brethren, whatsoever things are true, whatsoever things are honest, whatsoever things are just, whatsoever things are pure, whatsoever things are lovely, whatsoever things are of good report; if there be any virtue, and if there be any praise, think on these things.*

1 Corinthians 9:24 -- Know ye not that they which run in a race run all, but one receiveth the prize? So run, that ye may obtain.
Hebrews 10:23 -- Let us hold fast the profession of our faith

without wavering; (for he is faithful that promised;)

Hebrews 12:11-12 -- Now no chastening for the present seemeth to be joyous, but grievous: nevertheless afterward it yieldeth the peaceable fruit of righteousness unto them which are exercised thereby. Wherefore lift up the hands which hang down, and the feeble knees;

Matthew 7:7-8 -- Ask, and it shall be given you; seek, and ye shall find; knock, and it shall be opened unto you: For every one that asketh receiveth; and he that seeketh findeth; and to him that knocketh it shall be opened.

Philippians 3:14 -- I press toward the mark for the prize of the high calling of God in Christ Jesus.

Success

James 1:5 -- *If any of you lack wisdom, let him ask of God, that giveth to all men liberally, and upbraideth not; and it shall be given him.*

2 Timothy 1:7 -- For God hath not given us the spirit of fear; but of power, and of love, and of a sound mind.

Isaiah 30:21 -- And thine ears shall hear a word behind thee, saying, This is the way, walk ye in it, when ye turn to the right hand, and when ye turn to the left.

Jeremiah 33:3 -- Call unto me, and I will answer thee, and shew thee great and mighty things, which thou knowest not.

Proverbs 2:6-7 -- For the LORD giveth wisdom: out of his mouth cometh knowledge and understanding. He layeth up sound wisdom for the righteous: he is a buckler to them that walk uprightly.

Proverbs 28:5 -- Evil men understand not judgment: but they that seek the LORD understand all things.

Psalm 16:7 -- I will bless the LORD, who hath given me counsel: my reins also instruct me in the night seasons.

Psalm 32:8 -- I will instruct thee and teach thee in the way which thou shalt go: I will guide thee with mine eye.

Psalm 51:6 -- Behold, thou desirest truth in the inward parts: and in the hidden part thou shalt make me to know wisdom.

HEALTH

Physical Liberty

Luke 4:18 -- *The Spirit of the Lord is upon me, because he hath anointed me to preach the gospel to the poor; he hath sent me to heal the brokenhearted, to preach deliverance to the captives, and recovering of sight to the blind, to set at liberty them that are bruised,*

1 Chronicles 4:10 -- And Jabez called on the God of Israel, saying, Oh that thou wouldest bless me indeed, and enlarge my coast, and that thine hand might be with me, and that thou wouldest keep me from evil, that it may not grieve me! And God granted him that which he requested.

2 Samuel 22:2 -- And he said, The LORD is my rock, and my fortress, and my deliverer;

Deuteronomy 28:1-2 -- And it shall come to pass, if thou shalt hearken diligently unto the voice of the LORD thy God, to observe and to do all his commandments which I command thee this day, that the LORD thy God will set thee on high above all nations of the earth: And all these blessings shall come on thee, and overtake thee, if thou shalt hearken unto the voice of the LORD thy God.

Deuteronomy 28:7-9 -- The LORD shall cause thine enemies that rise up against thee to be smitten before thy face: they shall come out against thee one way, and flee before thee seven ways. The LORD shall command the blessing upon thee in thy storehouses, and in all that thou settest thine hand unto; and he shall bless thee in the land which the LORD thy God giveth thee. The LORD shall establish thee an holy people unto himself, as he hath sworn unto thee, if thou shalt keep the commandments of the LORD thy God, and walk in his ways.

Deuteronomy 28:12-14 -- The LORD shall open unto thee his good treasure, the heaven to give the rain unto thy land in his season, and to bless all the work of thine hand: and thou shalt lend unto many nations, and thou shalt not borrow. And the LORD shall make thee the head, and not the tail; and thou shalt be above only, and thou shalt not be beneath; if that thou hearken unto the commandments of the LORD thy God, which I command thee this day, to observe and to do them: And thou shalt not go aside from any of the words which I command thee this day, to the right hand, or to the left, to go after other gods to serve them.

Isaiah 49:25 -- But thus saith the LORD, Even the captives of the mighty shall be taken away, and the prey of the terrible shall be delivered: for I will contend with him that contendeth with thee, and I will save thy children.

Joel 2:32 -- And it shall come to pass, that whosoever shall call on the name of the LORD shall be delivered: for in mount Zion and in Jerusalem shall be deliverance, as the LORD hath said, and in the remnant whom the LORD shall call.

Matthew 11:28 -- Come unto me, all ye that labour and are heavy laden, and I will give you rest.

Proverbs 11:8 -- The righteous is delivered out of trouble, and the wicked cometh in his stead.

Psalm 22:4 -- Our fathers trusted in thee: they trusted, and thou didst deliver them.

Psalm 32:7 -- Thou art my hiding place; thou shalt preserve me from trouble; thou shalt compass me about with songs of deliverance. Selah.

Psalm 144:2 -- My goodness, and my fortress; my high tower, and my deliverer; my shield, and he in whom I trust; who subdueth my people under me.

Breaking Strongholds

Isaiah 10:27 -- *And it shall come to pass in that day,*
that his burden shall be taken away from off thy shoulder,
and his yoke from off thy neck, and the yoke shall
be destroyed because of the anointing.

1 John 4:4 -- Ye are of God, little children, and have overcome them: because greater is he that is in you, than he that is in the world.

1 John 5:4 -- For whatsoever is born of God overcometh the world: and this is the victory that overcometh the world, even our faith.

2 Corinthians 10:4-5 -- (For the weapons of our warfare are not carnal, but mighty through God to the pulling down of strong holds;) Casting down imaginations, and every high thing that exalteth itself against the knowledge of God, and bringing into captivity every thought to the obedience of Christ;

2 Timothy 1:7 -- For God hath not given us the spirit of fear; but of power, and of love, and of a sound mind.

Ephesians 6:12 -- For we wrestle not against flesh and blood, but against principalities, against powers, against the rulers of the darkness of this world, against spiritual wickedness in high places.

Isaiah 54:17 -- No weapon that is formed against thee shall prosper; and every tongue that shall rise against thee in judgment thou shalt condemn. This is the heritage of the servants of the LORD, and their righteousness is of me, saith the LORD.

John 16:33 -- These things I have spoken unto you, that in me ye might have peace. In the world ye shall have tribulation: but be of good cheer; I have overcome the world.

Luke 10:19 -- Behold, I give unto you power to tread on serpents and scorpions, and over all the power of the enemy: and nothing shall by any means hurt you.

Revelations 2:26 -- And he that overcometh, and keepeth my works unto the end, to him will I give power over the nations:

Revelations 3:5 -- He that overcometh, the same shall be clothed in white raiment; and I will not blot out his name out of the book of life, but I will confess his name before my Father, and before his angels.

Revelations 21:7 -- He that overcometh shall inherit all things; and I will be his God, and he shall be my son.

Deliverance

Joel 2:32 -- And it shall come to pass, that whosoever shall call on the name of the LORD shall be delivered: for in mount Zion and in Jerusalem shall be deliverance, as the LORD hath said, and in the remnant whom the LORD shall call.

1 Corinthians 15:57 -- But thanks be to God, which giveth us the victory through our Lord Jesus Christ.

1 John 2:20 -- But ye have an unction from the Holy One, and ye know all things.

2 Timothy 2:7 -- Consider what I say; and the Lord give thee understanding in all things.

Isaiah 30:21 -- And thine ears shall hear a word behind thee, saying, This is the way, walk ye in it, when ye turn to the right hand, and when ye turn to the left.

Isaiah 54:17 -- No weapon that is formed against thee shall prosper; and every tongue that shall rise against thee in judgment thou shalt condemn. This is the heritage of the servants of the LORD, and their righteousness is of me, saith the LORD.

Jeremiah 33:3 -- Call unto me, and I will answer thee, and shew thee great and mighty things, which thou knowest not.

Matthew 19:26 -- But Jesus beheld them, and said unto them, With men this is impossible; but with God all things are possible.

Proverbs 3:5 -- Trust in the LORD with all thine heart; and lean not unto thine own understanding.

Proverbs 3:6 -- In all thy ways acknowledge him, and he shall direct thy paths.

Proverbs 3:13 -- Happy is the man that findeth wisdom, and the man that getteth understanding.

Proverbs 4:18 -- But the path of the just is as the shining light, that shineth more and more unto the perfect day.

Psalm 18:30 -- As for God, his way is perfect: the word of the LORD is tried: he is a buckler to all those that trust in him.

Psalm 22:5 -- They cried unto thee, and were delivered: they trusted in thee, and were not confounded.

Psalm 32:8 -- I will instruct thee and teach thee in the way which thou shalt go: I will guide thee with mine eye.

Psalm 36:9 -- For with thee is the fountain of life: in thy light shall we see light.

Psalm 119:125 -- I am thy servant; give me understanding, that I may know thy testimonies.

Psalm 119:130 -- The entrance of thy words giveth light; it giveth understanding unto the simple.

Psalm 119:169 -- Let my cry come near before thee, O LORD: give me understanding according to thy word.

Romans 8:31 -- What shall we then say to these things? If God be for us, who can be against us?

Health and Healing

Jeremiah 17:14 -- *Heal me, O LORD, and I shall be healed; save me, and I shall be saved: for thou art my praise.*

1 John 4:4 -- Ye are of God, little children, and have overcome them: because greater is he that is in you, than he that is in the world.

1 Peter 5:10 -- But the God of all grace, who hath called us unto his eternal glory by Christ Jesus, after that ye have suffered a while, make you perfect, stablish, strengthen, settle you.

2 Timothy 1:7 -- For God hath not given us the spirit of fear; but of power, and of love, and of a sound mind.

3 John 1:2 -- Beloved, I wish above all things that thou mayest prosper and be in health, even as thy soul prospereth.

Exodus 23:25 -- And ye shall serve the LORD your God, and he shall bless thy bread, and thy water; and I will take sickness away from the midst of thee.

Isaiah 53:4-5 -- Surely he hath borne our griefs, and carried our sorrows: yet we did esteem him stricken, smitten of God, and afflicted. But he was wounded for our transgressions, he was bruised for our iniquities: the chastisement of our peace was upon him; and with his stripes we are healed.

Isaiah 54:7 -- For a small moment have I forsaken thee; but with great mercies will I gather thee.

Isaiah 55:11 -- So shall my word be that goeth forth out of my mouth: it shall not return unto me void, but it shall accomplish that which I please, and it shall prosper in the thing whereto I sent it.

Isaiah 58:12 -- And they that shall be of thee shall build the old waste places: thou shalt raise up the foundations of many generations; and thou shalt be called, The repairer of the breach, The restorer of paths to dwell in.

James 5:14-15 -- Is any sick among you? let him call for the elders of the church; and let them pray over him, anointing him with oil in the name of the Lord: And the prayer of faith shall save the sick, and the Lord shall raise him up; and if he have committed sins, they shall be forgiven him.

Jeremiah 30:17 -- For I will restore health unto thee, and I will heal thee of thy wounds, saith the LORD; because they called thee an Outcast, saying, This is Zion, whom no man seeketh after.

John 16:20 -- Verily, verily, I say unto you, That ye shall weep and lament, but the world shall rejoice: and ye shall be sorrowful, but your sorrow shall be turned into joy.

Mark 11:23-24 -- For verily I say unto you, That whosoever shall say unto this mountain, Be thou removed, and be thou cast into the sea; and shall not doubt in his heart, but shall believe that those things which he saith shall come to pass; he shall have whatsoever he saith. Therefore I say unto you, What things soever ye desire, when ye pray, believe that ye receive them, and ye shall have them.

Psalm 23:3 -- He restoreth my soul: he leadeth me in the paths of righteousness for his name's sake.

Psalm 91:16 -- With long life will I satisfy him, and shew him my salvation.

Psalm 102:2 -- Hide not thy face from me in the day when I am in trouble; incline thine ear unto me: in the day when I call answer me speedily.

Psalm 103:2-3 -- Bless the LORD, O my soul, and forget not all his benefits: Who forgiveth all thine iniquities; who healeth all thy diseases;

Psalm 107:20 -- He sent his word, and healed them, and delivered them from their destructions.

Psalm 119:76 -- Let, I pray thee, thy merciful kindness be for my comfort, according to thy word unto thy servant.

Mental and Physical Strength
Isaiah 40:31 -- But they that wait upon the LORD
shall renew their strength; they shall mount up
with wings as eagles; they shall run,
and not be weary; and they shall walk, and not faint.

1 Samuel 2:9 -- He will keep the feet of his saints, and the wicked shall be silent in darkness; for by strength shall no man prevail.

Isaiah 40:29 -- He giveth power to the faint; and to them that have no might he increaseth strength.

Isaiah 41:10 -- Fear thou not; for I am with thee: be not dismayed; for I am thy God: I will strengthen thee; yea, I will help thee; yea, I will uphold thee with the right hand of my righteousness.

John 14:1 -- Let not your heart be troubled: ye believe in God, believe also in me.

John 14:27 -- Peace I leave with you, my peace I give unto you: not as the world giveth, give I unto you. Let not your heart be troubled, neither let it be afraid.

Philippians 4:6-7 -- Be careful for nothing; but in every thing by prayer and supplication with thanksgiving let your requests be made known unto God. And the peace of God, which passeth all understanding, shall keep your hearts and minds through Christ Jesus.

Proverbs 3:24 -- When thou liest down, thou shalt not be afraid: yea, thou shalt lie down, and thy sleep shall be sweet.

Psalm 18:2 -- The LORD is my rock, and my fortress, and my deliverer; my God, my strength, in whom I will trust; my buckler, and the horn of my salvation, and my high tower.

Psalm 27:3 -- Though an host should encamp against me, my heart shall not fear: though war should rise against me, in this will I be confident.

Psalm 27:5 -- For in the time of trouble he shall hide me in his pavilion: in the secret of his tabernacle shall he hide me; he shall set me up upon a rock.

Psalm 3:3 -- But thou, O LORD, art a shield for me; my glory, and the lifter up of mine head.

Psalm 5:3 -- My voice shalt thou hear in the morning, O LORD; in the morning will I direct my prayer unto thee, and will look up.

Psalm 73:26 -- My flesh and my heart faileth: but God is the strength of my heart, and my portion for ever.

Psalm 9:9 -- The LORD also will be a refuge for the oppressed, a refuge in times of trouble.

Rest
Matthew 11:28 -- Come unto me, all ye that labour and are heavy laden, and I will give you rest.

Jeremiah 30:10 -- Therefore fear thou not, O my servant Jacob, saith the LORD; neither be dismayed, O Israel: for, lo, I will save thee from afar, and thy seed from the land of their captivity; and Jacob shall return, and shall be in rest, and be quiet, and none shall make him afraid.

Job 3:17 -- There the wicked cease from troubling; and there the weary be at rest.

Matthew 11:29-30 -- Take my yoke upon you, and learn of me; for I am meek and lowly in heart: and ye shall find rest unto your souls. For my yoke is easy, and my burden is light.

Psalm 37:7 -- Rest in the LORD, and wait patiently for him: fret not thyself because of him who prospereth in his way, because of the man who bringeth wicked devices to pass.

Psalm 116:7 -- Return unto thy rest, O my soul; for the LORD hath dealt bountifully with thee.

Barrenness

Deuteronomy 7:14 -- *Thou shalt be blessed above all people: there shall not be male or female barren among you, or among your cattle.*

Exodus 23:26 -- There shall nothing cast their young, nor be barren, in thy land: the number of thy days I will fulfil.

Galatians 4:27 -- For it is written, Rejoice, thou barren that bearest not; break forth and cry, thou that travailest not: for the desolate hath many more children than she which hath an husband.

Isaiah 54:1 -- Sing, O barren, thou that didst not bear; break forth into singing, and cry aloud, thou that didst not travail with child: for more are the children of the desolate than the children of the married wife, saith the LORD.

Psalm 113:9 -- He maketh the barren woman to keep house, and to be a joyful mother of children. Praise ye the LORD.

Transition

Ecclesiastes 3:1 -- *To every thing there is a season, and a time to every purpose under the heaven:*

1 John 1:9 -- If we confess our sins, he is faithful and just to forgive us our sins, and to cleanse us from all unrighteousness.

2 Timothy 4:2 -- Preach the word; be instant in season, out of season; reprove, rebuke, exhort with all longsuffering and doctrine.

Daniel 2:21 -- And he changeth the times and the seasons: he removeth kings, and setteth up kings: he giveth wisdom unto the wise, and knowledge to them that know understanding:

Galatians 6:9 -- And let us not be weary in well doing: for in due season we shall reap, if we faint not.

Isaiah 40:31 -- But they that wait upon the LORD shall renew their strength; they shall mount up with wings as eagles; they shall run, and not be weary; and they shall walk, and not faint.

Jeremiah 5:24 -- Neither say they in their heart, Let us now fear the LORD our God, that giveth rain, both the former and the latter, in his season: he reserveth unto us the appointed weeks of the harvest.

Leviticus 26:4 -- Then I will give you rain in due season, and the land shall yield her increase, and the trees of the field shall yield their fruit.

Luke 12:42 -- And the Lord said, Who then is that faithful and wise steward, whom his lord shall make ruler over his household, to give them their portion of meat in due season?

Proverbs 15:23 -- A man hath joy by the answer of his mouth: and a word spoken in due season, how good is it!

Psalm 1:3 -- And he shall be like a tree planted by the rivers of water, that bringeth forth his fruit in his season; his leaf also shall not wither; and whatsoever he doeth shall prosper.

Self-esteem

Proverbs 14:26 -- *In the fear of the LORD is strong confidence: and his children shall have a place of refuge.*

1 John 5:4 -- For whatsoever is born of God overcometh the world: and this is the victory that overcometh the world, even our faith.

1 John 5:14 -- And this is the confidence that we have in him, that, if we ask any thing according to his will, he heareth us:

Hebrews 13:6 -- So that we may boldly say, The Lord is my helper, and I will not fear what man shall do unto me.

Isaiah 30:15 -- For thus saith the Lord GOD, the Holy One of Israel; In returning and rest shall ye be saved; in quietness and in confidence shall be your strength: and ye would not.

Isaiah 41:13 -- For I the LORD thy God will hold thy right hand, saying unto thee, Fear not; I will help thee.

Philippians 3:3 -- For we are the circumcision, which worship God in the spirit, and rejoice in Christ Jesus, and have no confidence in the flesh.

Proverbs 3:26 -- For the LORD shall be thy confidence, and shall keep thy foot from being taken.

Proverbs 28:1 -- The wicked flee when no man pursueth: but the righteous are bold as a lion.

Romans 8:26 -- Likewise the Spirit also helpeth our infirmities: for we know not what we should pray for as we ought: but the Spirit itself maketh intercession for us with groanings which cannot be uttered.

Romans 8:31 -- What shall we then say to these things? If God be for us, who can be against us?

Romans 8:37 -- Nay, in all these things we are more than conquerors through him that loved us.

Peace

Isaiah 32:18 -- *And my people shall dwell in a peaceable habitation, and in sure dwellings, and in quiet resting places;*

1 Samuel 25:6 -- And thus shall ye say to him that liveth in prosperity, Peace be both to thee, and peace be to thine house, and peace be unto all that thou hast.

2 Peter 1:2 -- Grace and peace be multiplied unto you through the knowledge of God, and of Jesus our Lord,

2 Peter 3:14 -- Wherefore, beloved, seeing that ye look for such things, be diligent that ye may be found of him in peace, without spot, and blameless.

Daniel 10:19 -- And said, O man greatly beloved, fear not: peace be unto thee, be strong, yea, be strong. And when he had spoken unto me, I was strengthened, and said, Let my lord speak; for thou hast strengthened me.

Leviticus 26:6 -- And I will give peace in the land, and ye shall lie down, and none shall make you afraid: and I will rid evil beasts out of the land, neither shall the sword go through your land.

Numbers 6:26 -- The LORD lift up his countenance upon thee, and give thee peace.

Numbers 25:12 -- Wherefore say, Behold, I give unto him my covenant of peace:

Philippians 4:7 -- And the peace of God, which passeth all understanding, shall keep your hearts and minds through Christ Jesus.

Proverbs 3:2 -- For length of days, and long life, and peace, shall they add to thee.

Psalm 4:8 -- I will both lay me down in peace, and sleep: for thou, LORD, only makest me dwell in safety.

Psalm 55:18 -- He hath delivered my soul in peace from the battle that was against me: for there were many with me.

Psalm 72:7 -- In his days shall the righteous flourish; and abundance of peace so long as the moon endureth.

Psalm 119:165 -- Great peace have they which love thy law: and nothing shall offend them.

Psalm 122:7 -- Peace be within thy walls, and prosperity within thy palaces.

Fear

*1 John 4:18 -- There is no fear in love; but perfect love casteth out
fear: because fear hath torment.
He that feareth is not made perfect in love.*

Hebrews 13:6 -- So that we may boldly say, The Lord is my
helper, and I will not fear what man shall do unto me.

Isaiah 54:14 -- In righteousness shalt thou be established: thou
shalt be far from oppression; for thou shalt not fear: and from terror;
for it shall not come near thee.

Mark 6:50 -- For they all saw him, and were troubled. And
immediately he talked with them, and saith unto them, Be of good
cheer: it is I; be not afraid.

Proverbs 4:23 -- Keep thy heart with all diligence; for out of it are
the issues of life.

Rejection

*1 John 3:1 -- Behold, what manner of love the Father hath
bestowed upon us, that we should be called the sons of God:
therefore the world knoweth us not, because it knew him not.*

1 Peter 1:6-7 -- Wherein ye greatly rejoice, though now for a
season, if need be, ye are in heaviness through manifold temptations:
That the trial of your faith, being much more precious than of gold that
perisheth, though it be tried with fire, might be found unto praise and
honour and glory at the appearing of Jesus Christ:

Ephesians 1:4-6 -- According as he hath chosen us in him before
the foundation of the world, that we should be holy and without blame
before him in love: Having predestinated us unto the adoption of
children by Jesus Christ to himself, according to the good pleasure of
his will, To the praise of the glory of his grace, wherein he hath made
us accepted in the beloved.

Isaiah 51:7-8 -- Hearken unto me, ye that know righteousness, the
people in whose heart is my law; fear ye not the reproach of men,
neither be ye afraid of their revilings. For the moth shall eat them up
like a garment, and the worm shall eat them like wool: but my
righteousness shall be for ever, and my salvation from generation to
generation.

Proverbs 18:24 -- A man that hath friends must shew himself friendly: and there is a friend that sticketh closer than a brother.

Mistakes

Job 22:23 -- If thou return to the Almighty, thou shalt be built up, thou shalt put away iniquity far from thy tabernacles.

1 Corinthians 15:57 -- But thanks be to God, which giveth us the victory through our Lord Jesus Christ.

1 John 5:4 -- For whatsoever is born of God overcometh the world: and this is the victory that overcometh the world, even our faith.

2 Corinthians 2:14 -- Now thanks be unto God, which always causeth us to triumph in Christ, and maketh manifest the savour of his knowledge by us in every place.

Deuteronomy 4:29 -- But if from thence thou shalt seek the LORD thy God, thou shalt find him, if thou seek him with all thy heart and with all thy soul.

Deuteronomy 4:31 -- (For the LORD thy God is a merciful God;) he will not forsake thee, neither destroy thee, nor forget the covenant of thy fathers which he sware unto them.

Joel 2:25 -- And I will restore to you the years that the locust hath eaten, the cankerworm, and the caterpiller, and the palmerworm, my great army which I sent among you.

Matthew 19:26 -- But Jesus beheld them, and said unto them, With men this is impossible; but with God all things are possible.

Psalm 92:4 -- For thou, LORD, hast made me glad through thy work: I will triumph in the works of thy hands.

Revelations 21:7 -- He that overcometh shall inherit all things; and I will be his God, and he shall be my son.

Romans 8:31-32 -- What shall we then say to these things? If God be for us, who can be against us? He that spared not his own Son, but delivered him up for us all, how shall he not with him also freely give us all things?

Romans 8:35-37 -- Who shall separate us from the love of Christ? shall tribulation, or distress, or persecution, or famine, or nakedness, or peril, or sword? As it is written, For thy sake we are killed all the day long; we are accounted as sheep for the slaughter. Nay, in all these things we are more than conquerors through him that loved us.

Guilt

*Romans 8:1 -- There is therefore now no condemnation
to them which are in Christ Jesus,
who walk not after the flesh, but after the Spirit.*

1 John 1:7 -- But if we walk in the light, as he is in the light, we have fellowship one with another, and the blood of Jesus Christ his Son cleanseth us from all sin.

1 John 1:9 -- If we confess our sins, he is faithful and just to forgive us our sins, and to cleanse us from all unrighteousness.

Hebrews 8:12 -- For I will be merciful to their unrighteousness, and their sins and their iniquities will I remember no more.

Isaiah 1:18 -- Come now, and let us reason together, saith the LORD: though your sins be as scarlet, they shall be as white as snow; though they be red like crimson, they shall be as wool.

Isaiah 43:25 -- I, even I, am he that blotteth out thy transgressions for mine own sake, and will not remember thy sins.

Isaiah 55:7 -- Let the wicked forsake his way, and the unrighteous man his thoughts: and let him return unto the LORD, and he will have mercy upon him; and to our God, for he will abundantly pardon.

Jeremiah 33:8 -- And I will cleanse them from all their iniquity, whereby they have sinned against me; and I will pardon all their iniquities, whereby they have sinned, and whereby they have transgressed against me.

Psalm 51:17 -- The sacrifices of God are a broken spirit: a broken and a contrite heart, O God, thou wilt not despise.

Psalm 51:9 -- Hide thy face from my sins, and blot out all mine iniquities.

Psalm 103:12 -- As far as the east is from the west, so far hath he removed our transgressions from us.

Psalm 130:4 -- But there is forgiveness with thee, that thou mayest be feared.

Persecution

Zechariah 2:8 -- *For thus saith the LORD of hosts; After the glory hath he sent me unto the nations which spoiled you: for he that toucheth you toucheth the apple of his eye.*

1 Corinthians 4:12 -- And labour, working with our own hands: being reviled, we bless; being persecuted, we suffer it:

2 Corinthians 4:9 -- Persecuted, but not forsaken; cast down, but not destroyed;

2 Timothy 3:12 -- Yea, and all that will live godly in Christ Jesus shall suffer persecution.

John 15:20 -- Remember the word that I said unto you, The servant is not greater than his lord. If they have persecuted me, they will also persecute you; if they have kept my saying, they will keep yours also.

John 16:3 -- And these things will they do unto you, because they have not known the Father, nor me.

Matthew 5:12 -- Rejoice, and be exceeding glad: for great is your reward in heaven: for so persecuted they the prophets which were before you.

Romans 12:14 -- Bless them which persecute you: bless, and curse not.

Romans 8:35-39 -- Who shall separate us from the love of Christ? shall tribulation, or distress, or persecution, or famine, or nakedness, or peril, or sword? As it is written, For thy sake we are killed all the day long; we are accounted as sheep for the slaughter. Nay, in all these things we are more than conquerors through him that loved us. For I am persuaded, that neither death, nor life, nor angels, nor principalities, nor powers, nor things present, nor things to come, Nor height, nor depth, nor any other creature, shall be able to separate us from the love of God, which is in Christ Jesus our Lord.

Addictions and Compulsions

Psalm 107:6 -- *Then they cried unto the LORD in their trouble, and he delivered them out of their distresses.*

1 John 1:9 -- If we confess our sins, he is faithful and just to forgive us our sins, and to cleanse us from all unrighteousness.

Isaiah 55:6-7 -- Seek ye the LORD while he may be found, call ye upon him while he is near: Let the wicked forsake his way, and the unrighteous man his thoughts: and let him return unto the LORD, and he will have mercy upon him; and to our God, for he will abundantly pardon.

Proverbs 28:13 -- He that covereth his sins shall not prosper: but whoso confesseth and forsaketh them shall have mercy.

Proverbs 28:26 -- He that trusteth in his own heart is a fool: but whoso walketh wisely, he shall be delivered.

Psalm 34:14 -- Depart from evil, and do good; seek peace, and pursue it.

Psalm 55:18 -- He hath delivered my soul in peace from the battle that was against me: for there were many with me.

Psalm 107:20 -- He sent his word, and healed them, and delivered them from their destructions.

Discouragement

Isaiah 43:2 -- When thou passest through the waters,
I will be with thee; and through the rivers, they shall not overflow thee:
when thou walkest through the fire, thou shalt not be burned;
neither shall the flame kindle upon thee.

Hebrews 6:12 -- That ye be not slothful, but followers of them who through faith and patience inherit the promises.

Isaiah 51:3 -- For the LORD shall comfort Zion: he will comfort all her waste places; and he will make her wilderness like Eden, and her desert like the garden of the LORD; joy and gladness shall be found therein, thanksgiving, and the voice of melody.

Isaiah 51:12 -- I, even I, am he that comforteth you: who art thou, that thou shouldest be afraid of a man that shall die, and of the son of man which shall be made as grass;

Joshua 1:9 -- Have not I commanded thee? Be strong and of a good courage; be not afraid, neither be thou dismayed: for the LORD thy God is with thee whithersoever thou goest.

Philippians 1:6 -- Being confident of this very thing, that he which hath begun a good work in you will perform it until the day of Jesus Christ:

Psalm 37:3-5 -- Trust in the LORD, and do good; so shalt thou dwell in the land, and verily thou shalt be fed. Delight thyself also in the LORD; and he shall give thee the desires of thine heart. Commit thy way unto the LORD; trust also in him; and he shall bring it to pass.

Psalm 66:8-9 -- O bless our God, ye people, and make the voice of his praise to be heard: Which holdeth our soul in life, and suffereth not our feet to be moved.

Psalm 69:30 -- I will praise the name of God with a song, and will magnify him with thanksgiving.

Psalm 69:32 -- The humble shall see this, and be glad: and your heart shall live that seek God.

Psalm 73:23 -- Nevertheless I am continually with thee: thou hast holden me by my right hand.

Psalm 103:17 -- But the mercy of the LORD is from everlasting to everlasting upon them that fear him, and his righteousness unto children's children;

Psalm 138:3 -- In the day when I cried thou answeredst me, and strengthenedst me with strength in my soul.

Psalm 138:7-8 -- Though I walk in the midst of trouble, thou wilt revive me: thou shalt stretch forth thine hand against the wrath of mine enemies, and thy right hand shall save me. The LORD will perfect that which concerneth me: thy mercy, O LORD, endureth for ever: forsake not the works of thine own hands.

Sadness

Isaiah 61:3 -- *To appoint unto them that mourn in Zion, to give unto them beauty for ashes, the oil of joy for mourning, the garment of praise for the spirit of heaviness; that they might be called trees of righteousness, the planting of the LORD, that he might be glorified.*

1 Kings 1:40 -- And all the people came up after him, and the people piped with pipes, and rejoiced with great joy, so that the earth rent with the sound of them.

Ecclesiastes 9:7 -- Go thy way, eat thy bread with joy, and drink thy wine with a merry heart; for God now accepteth thy works.

Isaiah 29:19 -- The meek also shall increase their joy in the LORD, and the poor among men shall rejoice in the Holy One of Israel.

Isaiah 55:12 -- For ye shall go out with joy, and be led forth with peace: the mountains and the hills shall break forth before you into singing, and all the trees of the field shall clap their hands.

Jeremiah 15:16 -- Thy words were found, and I did eat them; and thy word was unto me the joy and rejoicing of mine heart: for I am called by thy name, O LORD God of hosts.

Proverbs 23:24 -- The father of the righteous shall greatly rejoice: and he that begetteth a wise child shall have joy of him.

Psalm 42:4 -- When I remember these things, I pour out my soul in me: for I had gone with the multitude, I went with them to the house of God, with the voice of joy and praise, with a multitude that kept holyday.

Psalm 43:4 -- Then will I go unto the altar of God, unto God my exceeding joy: yea, upon the harp will I praise thee, O God my God.

Bitterness

Colossians 3:13 -- *Forbearing one another,*
and forgiving one another, if any man have a
quarrel against any: even as Christ forgave you, so also do ye.

Ephesians 4:31 -- Let all bitterness, and wrath, and anger, and clamour, and evil speaking, be put away from you, with all malice:

Hebrews 12:15 -- Looking diligently lest any man fail of the grace of God; lest any root of bitterness springing up trouble you, and thereby many be defiled;

Isaiah 38:17 -- Behold, for peace I had great bitterness: but thou hast in love to my soul delivered it from the pit of corruption: for thou hast cast all my sins behind thy back.

James 3:13-16 -- Who is a wise man and endued with knowledge among you? let him shew out of a good conversation his works with meekness of wisdom. But if ye have bitter envying and strife in your hearts, glory not, and lie not against the truth. This wisdom descendeth not from above, but is earthly, sensual, devilish. For where envying and strife is, there is confusion and every evil work.

Proverbs 10:12 -- Hatred stirreth up strifes: but love covereth all sins.

Emotional Damage

Revelations 21:4 -- *And God shall wipe away all tears from their eyes; and there shall be no more death, neither sorrow, nor crying, neither shall there be any more pain: for the former things are passed away*

1 Peter 3:14-15 -- But and if ye suffer for righteousness' sake, happy are ye: and be not afraid of their terror, neither be troubled; But sanctify the Lord God in your hearts: and be ready always to give an answer to every man that asketh you a reason of the hope that is in you with meekness and fear:

Deuteronomy 15:10 -- Thou shalt surely give him, and thine heart shall not be grieved when thou givest unto him: because that for this thing the LORD thy God shall bless thee in all thy works, and in all that thou puttest thine hand unto.

Isaiah 35:10 -- And the ransomed of the LORD shall return, and come to Zion with songs and everlasting joy upon their heads: they shall obtain joy and gladness, and sorrow and sighing shall flee away.

Isaiah 53:4 -- Surely he hath borne our griefs, and carried our sorrows: yet we did esteem him stricken, smitten of God, and afflicted.

Job 41:22 -- In his neck remaineth strength, and sorrow is turned into joy before him.

Matthew 10:26 -- Fear them not therefore: for there is nothing covered, that shall not be revealed; and hid, that shall not be known.

Proverbs 10:22 -- The blessing of the LORD, it maketh rich, and he addeth no sorrow with it.

Psalm 72:4 -- He shall judge the poor of the people, he shall save the children of the needy, and shall break in pieces the oppressor.

Psalm 74:21 -- O let not the oppressed return ashamed: let the poor and needy praise thy name.

Psalm 78:53 -- And he led them on safely, so that they feared not: but the sea overwhelmed their enemies.

Psalm 9:9 -- The LORD also will be a refuge for the oppressed, a refuge in times of trouble.

Psalm 119:134 -- Deliver me from the oppression of man: so will I keep thy precepts.

Psalm 127:2 -- It is vain for you to rise up early, to sit up late, to eat the bread of sorrows: for so he giveth his beloved sleep.

Frustration

Hebrews 4:9-11 -- *There remaineth therefore a rest to the people of God. For he that is entered into his rest, he also hath ceased from his own works, as God did from his. Let us labour therefore to enter into that rest, lest any man fall after the same example of unbelief.*

1 John 5:4 -- For whatsoever is born of God overcometh the world: and this is the victory that overcometh the world, even our faith.

1 John 5:14 -- And this is the confidence that we have in him, that, if we ask any thing according to his will, he heareth us:

Colossians 3:15 -- And let the peace of God rule in your hearts, to the which also ye are called in one body; and be ye thankful.

Isaiah 26:4 -- Trust ye in the LORD for ever: for in the LORD JEHOVAH is everlasting strength:

Isaiah 30:15 -- For thus saith the Lord GOD, the Holy One of Israel; In returning and rest shall ye be saved; in quietness and in confidence shall be your strength: and ye would not.

Isaiah 41:13 -- For I the LORD thy God will hold thy right hand, saying unto thee, Fear not; I will help thee.

John 8:31 -- Then said Jesus to those Jews which believed on him, If ye continue in my word, then are ye my disciples indeed;

Philippians 3:3 -- For we are the circumcision, which worship God in the spirit, and rejoice in Christ Jesus, and have no confidence in the flesh.

Philippians 4:13 -- I can do all things through Christ which strengtheneth me.

Proverbs 3:26 -- For the LORD shall be thy confidence, and shall keep thy foot from being taken.

Proverbs 16:3 -- Commit thy works unto the LORD, and thy thoughts shall be established.

Psalm 27:13-14 -- I had fainted, unless I had believed to see the goodness of the LORD in the land of the living. Wait on the LORD: be of good courage, and he shall strengthen thine heart: wait, I say, on the LORD.

Psalm 32:6 -- For this shall every one that is godly pray unto thee in a time when thou mayest be found: surely in the floods of great waters they shall not come nigh unto him.

Psalm 32:8 -- I will instruct thee and teach thee in the way which thou shalt go: I will guide thee with mine eye.

Romans 8:26 -- Likewise the Spirit also helpeth our infirmities: for we know not what we should pray for as we ought: but the Spirit itself maketh intercession for us with groanings which cannot be uttered.

Romans 8:31 -- What shall we then say to these things? If God be for us, who can be against us?

Romans 14:19 -- Let us therefore follow after the things which make for peace, and things wherewith one may edify another.

Insecurity

Psalm 27:3 -- *Though an host should encamp against me, my heart shall not fear: though war should rise against me, in this will I be confident.*

2 Corinthians 5:6 -- Therefore we are always confident, knowing that, whilst we are at home in the body, we are absent from the Lord:

Isaiah 30:15 -- For thus saith the Lord GOD, the Holy One of Israel; In returning and rest shall ye be saved; in quietness and in confidence shall be your strength: and ye would not.

Philippians 1:6 -- Being confident of this very thing, that he which hath begun a good work in you will perform it until the day of Jesus Christ:

Proverbs 3:26 -- For the LORD shall be thy confidence, and shall keep thy foot from being taken.

Psalm 118:8 -- It is better to trust in the LORD than to put confidence in man.

Intimidation

1 John 4:4 -- *Ye are of God, little children, and have overcome them: because greater is he that is in you, than he that is in the world*

Hebrews 13:5 -- Let your conversation be without covetousness; and be content with such things as ye have: for he hath said, I will never leave thee, nor forsake thee.

Isaiah 26:3 -- Thou wilt keep him in perfect peace, whose mind is stayed on thee: because he trusteth in thee.

John 8:32 -- And ye shall know the truth, and the truth shall make you free.

John 16:33 -- These things I have spoken unto you, that in me ye might have peace. In the world ye shall have tribulation: but be of good cheer; I have overcome the world.

Philippians 4:13 -- I can do all things through Christ which strengtheneth me.

.

Jealousy

Proverbs 14:30 -- A sound heart is the life of the flesh: but envy the rottenness of the bones.

Deuteronomy 5:21 -- Neither shalt thou desire thy neighbour's wife, neither shalt thou covet thy neighbour's house, his field, or his manservant, or his maidservant, his ox, or his ass, or any thing that is thy neighbour's.

James 3:14 -- But if ye have bitter envying and strife in your hearts, glory not, and lie not against the truth.

James 3:16 -- For where envying and strife is, there is confusion and every evil work.

Philippians 4:8 -- Finally, brethren, whatsoever things are true, whatsoever things are honest, whatsoever things are just, whatsoever things are pure, whatsoever things are lovely, whatsoever things are of good report; if there be any virtue, and if there be any praise, think on these things.

Proverbs 3:31 -- Envy thou not the oppressor, and choose none of his ways.

Proverbs 23:17 -- Let not thine heart envy sinners: but be thou in the fear of the LORD all the day long.

Proverbs 24:1 -- Be not thou envious against evil men, neither desire to be with them.

Psalm 37:7 -- Rest in the LORD, and wait patiently for him: fret not thyself because of him who prospereth in his way, because of the man who bringeth wicked devices to pass.

Psalm 51:7 -- Purge me with hyssop, and I shall be clean: wash me, and I shall be whiter than snow.

Psalm 51:10 -- Create in me a clean heart, O God; and renew a right spirit within me.

Loneliness

Hebrews 13:5 -- *Let your conversation be without covetousness;*
and be content with such things as ye have:
for he hath said, I will never leave thee, nor forsake thee.

John 10:27 -- My sheep hear my voice, and I know them, and they follow me:

Joshua 1:5 -- There shall not any man be able to stand before thee all the days of thy life: as I was with Moses, so I will be with thee: I will not fail thee, nor forsake thee.

Matthew 18:20 -- For where two or three are gathered together in my name, there am I in the midst of them.

Matthew 28:20 -- Teaching them to observe all things whatsoever I have commanded you: and, lo, I am with you alway, even unto the end of the world. Amen.

Proverbs 18:24 -- A man that hath friends must shew himself friendly: and there is a friend that sticketh closer than a brother.

Anger

Matthew 5:9 -- *Blessed are the peacemakers:*
for they shall be called the children of God.

1 Corinthians 13:4-5 -- Charity suffereth long, and is kind; charity envieth not; charity vaunteth not itself, is not puffed up, Doth not behave itself unseemly, seeketh not her own, is not easily provoked, thinketh no evil;

2 Corinthians 10:4 -- (For the weapons of our warfare are not carnal, but mighty through God to the pulling down of strong holds;)

Ecclesiastes 7:9 -- Be not hasty in thy spirit to be angry: for anger resteth in the bosom of fools.

Ephesians 4:31 -- Let all bitterness, and wrath, and anger, and clamour, and evil speaking, be put away from you, with all malice:

Ephesians 6:10 -- Finally, my brethren, be strong in the Lord, and in the power of his might.

Galatians 5:22-23 -- But the fruit of the Spirit is love, joy, peace, longsuffering, gentleness, goodness, faith, Meekness, temperance: against such there is no law.

James 3:13 -- Who is a wise man and endued with knowledge among you? let him shew out of a good conversation his works with meekness of wisdom.

Proverbs 14:17 -- He that is soon angry dealeth foolishly: and a man of wicked devices is hated.

Proverbs 16:32 -- He that is slow to anger is better than the mighty; and he that ruleth his spirit than he that taketh a city.

Psalm 37:8 -- Cease from anger, and forsake wrath: fret not thyself in any wise to do evil.

Pride

1 Peter 5:6 -- Humble yourselves therefore under the mighty hand of God, that he may exalt you in due time.

1 Peter 5:5 -- Likewise, ye younger, submit yourselves unto the elder. Yea, all of you be subject one to another, and be clothed with humility: for God resisteth the proud, and giveth grace to the humble.

Isaiah 57:15 -- For thus saith the high and lofty One that inhabiteth eternity, whose name is Holy; I dwell in the high and holy place, with him also that is of a contrite and humble spirit, to revive the spirit of the humble, and to revive the heart of the contrite ones.

James 4:6-7 -- But he giveth more grace. Wherefore he saith, God resisteth the proud, but giveth grace unto the humble. Submit yourselves therefore to God. Resist the devil, and he will flee from you.

Matthew 23:11 -- But he that is greatest among you shall be your servant.

Proverbs 11:2 -- When pride cometh, then cometh shame: but with the lowly is wisdom.

Proverbs 21:4 -- An high look, and a proud heart, and the plowing of the wicked, is sin.

Proverbs 22:4 -- By humility and the fear of the LORD are riches, and honour, and life.

Romans 12:3 -- For I say, through the grace given unto me, to every man that is among you, not to think of himself more highly than he ought to think; but to think soberly, according as God hath dealt to every man the measure of faith.

Weariness & Burdens

John 14:16-18 -- *And I will pray the Father, and he shall give you another Comforter, that he may abide with you for ever; Even the Spirit of truth; whom the world cannot receive, because it seeth him not, neither knoweth him: but ye know him; for he dwelleth with you, and shall be in you. I will not leave you comfortless: I will come to you.*

1 John 4:18 -- There is no fear in love; but perfect love casteth out fear: because fear hath torment. He that feareth is not made perfect in love.

2 Peter 1:2 -- Grace and peace be multiplied unto you through the knowledge of God, and of Jesus our Lord,

2 Peter 3:14 -- Wherefore, beloved, seeing that ye look for such things, be diligent that ye may be found of him in peace, without spot, and blameless.

Exodus 33:14 -- And he said, My presence shall go with thee, and I will give thee rest.

Isaiah 26:12 -- LORD, thou wilt ordain peace for us: for thou also hast wrought all our works in us.

Isaiah 32:18 -- And my people shall dwell in a peaceable habitation, and in sure dwellings, and in quiet resting places;

Isaiah 48:18 -- O that thou hadst hearkened to my commandments! then had thy peace been as a river, and thy righteousness as the waves of the sea:

James 4:7 -- Submit yourselves therefore to God. Resist the devil, and he will flee from you.

Jeremiah 31:25 -- For I have satiated the weary soul, and I have replenished every sorrowful soul.

John 14:26-27 -- But the Comforter, which is the Holy Ghost, whom the Father will send in my name, he shall teach you all things, and bring all things to your remembrance, whatsoever I have said unto you. Peace I leave with you, my peace I give unto you: not as the world giveth, give I unto you. Let not your heart be troubled, neither let it be afraid.

Proverbs 3:2 -- For length of days, and long life, and peace, shall they add to thee.

Psalm 20:6 -- Now know I that the LORD saveth his anointed; he will hear him from his holy heaven with the saving strength of his right hand.

Psalm 39:13 -- O spare me, that I may recover strength, before I go hence, and be no more.

Psalm 46:1 -- ...God is our refuge and strength, a very present help in trouble.

Psalm 55:22 -- Cast thy burden upon the LORD, and he shall sustain thee: he shall never suffer the righteous to be moved.

Psalm 73:26 -- My flesh and my heart faileth: but God is the strength of my heart, and my portion for ever.

Psalm 116:7 -- Return unto thy rest, O my soul; for the LORD hath dealt bountifully with thee.

Psalm 127:2 -- It is vain for you to rise up early, to sit up late, to eat the bread of sorrows: for so he giveth his beloved sleep.

Comfort

John 14:26 -- But the Comforter, which is the Holy Ghost, whom the Father will send in my name, he shall teach you all things, and bring all things to your remembrance, whatsoever I have said unto you.

1 Peter 3:8 -- Finally, be ye all of one mind, having compassion one of another, love as brethren, be pitiful, be courteous:

2 Corinthians 1:3-4 -- Blessed be God, even the Father of our Lord Jesus Christ, the Father of mercies, and the God of all comfort; Who comforteth us in all our tribulation, that we may be able to comfort them which are in any trouble, by the comfort wherewith we ourselves are comforted of God.

2 Corinthians 1:6 -- And whether we be afflicted, it is for your consolation and salvation, which is effectual in the enduring of the same sufferings which we also suffer: or whether we be comforted, it is for your consolation and salvation.

2 Corinthians 13:11 -- Finally, brethren, farewell. Be perfect, be of good comfort, be of one mind, live in peace; and the God of love and peace shall be with you.

Isaiah 52:9 -- Break forth into joy, sing together, ye waste places of Jerusalem: for the LORD hath comforted his people, he hath redeemed Jerusalem.

Isaiah 57:18 -- I have seen his ways, and will heal him: I will lead him also, and restore comforts unto him and to his mourners.

Isaiah 66:13 -- As one whom his mother comforteth, so will I comfort you; and ye shall be comforted in Jerusalem.

John 14:18 -- I will not leave you comfortless: I will come to you.

Psalm 119:28 -- My soul melteth for heaviness: strengthen thou me according unto thy word.

Psalm 119:50 -- This is my comfort in my affliction: for thy word hath quickened me.

Psalm 119:67 -- Before I was afflicted I went astray: but now have I kept thy word.

Psalm 119:76 -- Let, I pray thee, thy merciful kindness be for my comfort, according to thy word unto thy servant.

Psalm 119:81-82 -- My soul fainteth for thy salvation: but I hope in thy word. Mine eyes fail for thy word, saying, When wilt thou comfort me?

Psalm 119:170 -- Let my supplication come before thee: deliver me according to thy word.

Psalm 119:175 -- Let my soul live, and it shall praise thee; and let thy judgments help me.

Zechariah 1:17 -- Cry yet, saying, Thus saith the LORD of hosts; My cities through prosperity shall yet be spread abroad; and the LORD shall yet comfort Zion, and shall yet choose Jerusalem.

Walking in Love
John 13:34-35 -- *A new commandment I give unto you,*
That ye love one another; as I have loved you,that ye also love one
another. By this shall all men knowthat ye are my disciples,
if ye have love one to another.

1 Corinthians 13:4 -- Charity suffereth long, and is kind; charity envieth not; charity vaunteth not itself, is not puffed up,

1 Corinthians 13:13 -- And now abideth faith, hope, charity, these three; but the greatest of these is charity.

1 John 3:18 -- My little children, let us not love in word, neither in tongue; but in deed and in truth.

1 John 4:10-12 -- Herein is love, not that we loved God, but that he loved us, and sent his Son to be the propitiation for our sins. Beloved, if God so loved us, we ought also to love one another. No man hath seen God at any time. If we love one another, God dwelleth in us, and his love is perfected in us.

1 John 4:7-8 -- Beloved, let us love one another: for love is of God; and every one that loveth is born of God, and knoweth God. He that loveth not knoweth not God; for God is love.

1 John 4:16-18 -- And we have known and believed the love that God hath to us. God is love; and he that dwelleth in love dwelleth in God, and God in him. Herein is our love made perfect, that we may have boldness in the day of judgment: because as he is, so are we in this world. There is no fear in love; but perfect love casteth out fear: because fear hath torment. He that feareth is not made perfect in love.

1 Peter 1:22 -- Seeing ye have purified your souls in obeying the truth through the Spirit unto unfeigned love of the brethren, see that ye love one another with a pure heart fervently:

1 Timothy 1:5 -- Now the end of the commandment is charity out of a pure heart, and of a good conscience, and of faith unfeigned:

Colossians 3:14 -- And above all these things put on charity, which is the bond of perfectness.

Ephesians 5:2 -- And walk in love, as Christ also hath loved us, and hath given himself for us an offering and a sacrifice to God for a sweet smelling savour.

Hebrews 10:24 -- And let us consider one another to provoke unto love and to good works:

Hebrews 13:1 -- Let brotherly love continue.

John 15:10 -- If ye keep my commandments, ye shall abide in my love; even as I have kept my Father's commandments, and abide in his love.

John 15:9 -- As the Father hath loved me, so have I loved you: continue ye in my love.

Leviticus 19:18 -- Thou shalt not avenge, nor bear any grudge against the children of thy people, but thou shalt love thy neighbour as thyself: I am the LORD.

Romans 8:35 -- Who shall separate us from the love of Christ? shall tribulation, or distress, or persecution, or famine, or nakedness, or peril, or sword?

Romans 12:9-10 -- Let love be without dissimulation. Abhor that which is evil; cleave to that which is good. Be kindly affectioned one to another with brotherly love; in honour preferring one another;

Romans 13:10 -- Love worketh no ill to his neighbour: therefore love is the fulfilling of the law.

Offences

Matthew 6:14 -- *For if ye forgive men their trespasses, your heavenly Father will also forgive you:*

1 Corinthians 13:4 -- Charity suffereth long, and is kind; charity envieth not; charity vaunteth not itself, is not puffed up,

2 Timothy 2:24 -- And the servant of the Lord must not strive; but be gentle unto all men, apt to teach, patient,

2 Timothy 4:17-18 -- Notwithstanding the Lord stood with me, and strengthened me; that by me the preaching might be fully known, and that all the Gentiles might hear: and I was delivered out of the mouth of the lion. And the Lord shall deliver me from every evil work, and will preserve me unto his heavenly kingdom: to whom be glory for ever and ever. Amen.

Colossians 3:8 -- But now ye also put off all these; anger, wrath, malice, blasphemy, filthy communication out of your mouth.

Leviticus 19:18 -- Thou shalt not avenge, nor bear any grudge against the children of thy people, but thou shalt love thy neighbour as thyself: I am the LORD.

Luke 17:4 -- And if he trespass against thee seven times in a day, and seven times in a day turn again to thee, saying, I repent; thou shalt forgive him.

Proverbs 20:22 -- Say not thou, I will recompense evil; but wait on the LORD, and he shall save thee.

Psalm 91:15 -- He shall call upon me, and I will answer him: I will be with him in trouble; I will deliver him, and honour him.

Psalm 94:14 -- For the LORD will not cast off his people, neither will he forsake his inheritance.

Romans 12:17 -- Recompense to no man evil for evil. Provide things honest in the sight of all men.

Temptation

1 Corinthians 10:13 -- There hath no temptation taken you but such as is common to man: but God is faithful, who will not suffer you to be tempted above that ye a re able; but will with the temptation also make a way to escape, that ye may be able to bear it.

1 Peter 2:11 -- Dearly beloved, I beseech you as strangers and pilgrims, abstain from fleshly lusts, which war against the soul;

1 Thessalonians 4:4 -- That every one of you should know how to possess his vessel in sanctification and honour;

Colossians 3:5 -- Mortify therefore your members which are upon the earth; fornication, uncleanness, inordinate affection, evil concupiscence, and covetousness, which is idolatry:

Ephesians 4:22 -- That ye put off concerning the former conversation the old man, which is corrupt according to the deceitful lusts;

James 1:13-15 -- Let no man say when he is tempted, I am tempted of God: for God cannot be tempted with evil, neither tempteth he any man: But every man is tempted, when he is drawn away of his own lust, and enticed. Then when lust hath conceived, it bringeth forth sin: and sin, when it is finished, bringeth forth death.

Matthew 26:41 -- Watch and pray, that ye enter not into temptation: the spirit indeed is willing, but the flesh is weak.

Proverbs 2:11 -- Discretion shall preserve thee, understanding shall keep thee:

Proverbs 4:14 -- Enter not into the path of the wicked, and go not in the way of evil men.

Proverbs 6:23 -- For the commandment is a lamp; and the law is light; and reproofs of instruction are the way of life:

Ungodly Relationships

Ephesians 5:8 -- *For ye were sometimes darkness, but now are ye light in the Lord: walk as children of light:*

1 Thessalonians 5:5 -- Ye are all the children of light, and the children of the day: we are not of the night, nor of darkness.

Isaiah 50:10 -- Who is among you that feareth the LORD, that obeyeth the voice of his servant, that walketh in darkness, and hath no light? let him trust in the name of the LORD, and stay upon his God.

Luke 11:34 -- The light of the body is the eye: therefore when thine eye is single, thy whole body also is full of light; but when thine eye is evil, thy body also is full of darkness.

Proverbs 11:30 -- The fruit of the righteous is a tree of life; and he that winneth souls is wise.

Proverbs 13:20 -- He that walketh with wise men shall be wise: but a companion of fools shall be destroyed.

Proverbs 28:7 -- Whoso keepeth the law is a wise son: but he that is a companion of riotous men shameth his father.

Psalm 119:63 -- I am a companion of all them that fear thee, and of them that keep thy precepts.

Romans 13:2 -- Whosoever therefore resisteth the power, resisteth the ordinance of God: and they that resist shall receive to themselves damnation.

Romans 16:17 -- Now I beseech you, brethren, mark them which cause divisions and offences contrary to the doctrine which ye have learned; and avoid them.

Abuse / Physical

John 10:10 -- *The thief cometh not, but for to steal,
and to kill, and to destroy: I am come that
they might have life, and that they might have it more abundantly*

Abuse / Emotional

Isaiah 35:10 -- *And the ransomed of the LORD
shall return, and come to Zion with songs and
everlasting joy upon their heads: they shall obtain
joy and gladness, and sorrow and sighing shall flee away.*

1 John 3:1-2 -- Behold, what manner of love the Father hath bestowed upon us, that we should be called the sons of God: therefore the world knoweth us not, because it knew him not. Beloved, now are we the sons of God, and it doth not yet appear what we shall be: but we know that, when he shall appear, we shall be like him; for we shall see him as he is.

1 Peter 3:14-15 -- But and if ye suffer for righteousness' sake, happy are ye: and be not afraid of their terror, neither be troubled; But sanctify the Lord God in your hearts: and be ready always to give an answer to every man that asketh you a reason of the hope that is in you with meekness and fear:

Isaiah 53:4 -- Surely he hath borne our griefs, and carried our sorrows: yet we did esteem him stricken, smitten of God, and afflicted.

Isaiah 54:6 -- For the LORD hath called thee as a woman forsaken and grieved in spirit, and a wife of youth, when thou wast refused, saith thy God.

Isaiah 61:1-3 -- The Spirit of the Lord GOD is upon me; because the LORD hath anointed me to preach good tidings unto the meek; he hath sent me to bind up the brokenhearted, to proclaim liberty to the captives, and the opening of the prison to them that are bound; To proclaim the acceptable year of the LORD, and the day of vengeance of our God; to comfort all that mourn; To appoint unto them that mourn in Zion, to give unto them beauty for ashes, the oil of joy for mourning, the garment of praise for the spirit of heaviness; that they might be called trees of righteousness, the planting of the LORD, that he might be glorified.

John 8:32 -- And ye shall know the truth, and the truth shall make you free.

Luke 13:11-12 -- And, behold, there was a woman which had a spirit of infirmity eighteen years, and was bowed together, and could in no wise lift up herself. And when Jesus saw her, he called her to him, and said unto her, Woman, thou art loosed from thine infirmity.

Matthew 5:44 -- But I say unto you, Love your enemies, bless them that curse you, do good to them that hate you, and pray for them which despitefully use you, and persecute you;

Matthew 10:26 -- Fear them not therefore: for there is nothing covered, that shall not be revealed; and hid, that shall not be known.

Matthew 10:28 -- And fear not them which kill the body, but are not able to kill the soul: but rather fear him which is able to destroy both soul and body in hell.

Philippians 1:6 -- Being confident of this very thing, that he which hath begun a good work in you will perform it until the day of Jesus Christ:

Philippians 3:13 -- Brethren, I count not myself to have apprehended: but this one thing I do, forgetting those things which are behind, and reaching forth unto those things which are before,

Psalm 9:9 -- The LORD also will be a refuge for the oppressed, a refuge in times of trouble.

Revelations 21:4 -- And God shall wipe away all tears from their eyes; and there shall be no more death, neither sorrow, nor crying, neither shall there be any more pain: for the former things are passed away.

Psalm 72:4 -- He shall judge the poor of the people, he shall save the children of the needy, and shall break in pieces the oppressor.

Psalm 74:21 -- O let not the oppressed return ashamed: let the poor and needy praise thy name.

Psalm 78:53 -- And he led them on safely, so that they feared not: but the sea overwhelmed their enemies.

Psalm 119:134 -- Deliver me from the oppression of man: so will I keep thy precepts.

Romans 6:4 -- Therefore we are buried with him by baptism into death: that like as Christ was raised up from the dead by the glory of the Father, even so we also should walk in newness of life.

Romans 8:2 -- For the law of the Spirit of life in Christ Jesus hath made me free from the law of sin and death.

INTERCESSION

Overcoming Strongholds

2 Timothy 2:26 -- And that they may recover themselves out of the snare of the devil, who are taken captive by him at his will.

Isaiah 41:11-12 -- Behold, all they that were incensed against thee shall be ashamed and confounded: they shall be as nothing; and they that strive with thee shall perish. Thou shalt seek them, and shalt not find them, even them that contended with thee: they that war against thee shall be as nothing, and as a thing of nought.

1 John 4:4 -- Ye are of God, little children, and have overcome them: because greater is he that is in you, than he that is in the world.

1 John 5:4 -- For whatsoever is born of God overcometh the world: and this is the victory that overcometh the world, even our faith.

2 Corinthians 10:4-5 -- (For the weapons of our warfare are not carnal, but mighty through God to the pulling down of strong holds;) Casting down imaginations, and every high thing that exalteth itself against the knowledge of God, and bringing into captivity every thought to the obedience of Christ;

2 Timothy 1:7 -- For God hath not given us the spirit of fear; but of power, and of love, and of a sound mind.

Colossians 2:15 -- And having spoiled principalities and powers, he made a shew of them openly, triumphing over them in it.

Ephesians 1:22 -- And hath put all things under his feet, and gave him to be the head over all things to the church,

Ephesians 4:27 -- Neither give place to the devil.

Ephesians 6:12 -- For we wrestle not against flesh and blood, but against principalities, against powers, against the rulers of the darkness of this world, against spiritual wickedness in high places.

Galatians 1:4 -- Who gave himself for our sins, that he might deliver us from this present evil world, according to the will of God and our Father:

Isaiah 45:16 -- They shall be ashamed, and also confounded, all of them: they shall go to confusion together that are makers of idols.

Isaiah 23:11 -- He stretched out his hand over the sea, he shook the kingdoms: the LORD hath given a commandment against the merchant city, to destroy the strong holds thereof.

Isaiah 54:17 -- No weapon that is formed against thee shall prosper; and every tongue that shall rise against thee in judgment thou shalt condemn. This is the heritage of the servants of the LORD, and their righteousness is of me, saith the LORD.

James 4:7 -- Submit yourselves therefore to God. Resist the devil, and he will flee from you.

John 8:36 -- If the Son therefore shall make you free, ye shall be free indeed.

Luke 10:19 -- Behold, I give unto you power to tread on serpents and scorpions, and over all the power of the enemy: and nothing shall by any means hurt you.

Mark 16:17 -- And these signs shall follow them that believe; In my name shall they cast out devils; they shall speak with new tongues;

Matthew 12:29 -- Or else how can one enter into a strong man's house, and spoil his goods, except he first bind the strong man? and then he will spoil his house.

Matthew 10:19 -- But when they deliver you up, take no thought how or what ye shall speak: for it shall be given you in that same hour what ye shall speak.

Nahum 1:7 -- The LORD is good, a strong hold in the day of trouble; and he knoweth them that trust in him.

Psalm 35:1-6 -- A Psalm of David. Plead my cause, O LORD, with them that strive with me: fight against them that fight against me. Take hold of shield and buckler, and stand up for mine help. Draw out also the spear, and stop the way against them that persecute me: say unto my soul, I am thy salvation. Let them be confounded and put to shame that seek after my soul: let them be turned back and brought to confusion that devise my hurt. Let them be as chaff before the wind: and let the angel of the LORD chase them. Let their way be dark and slippery: and let the angel of the LORD persecute them.

Psalm 35:8 -- Let destruction come upon him at unawares; and let his net that he hath hid catch himself: into that very destruction let him fall.

Psalm 89:40 -- Thou hast broken down all his hedges; thou hast brought his strong holds to ruin.

Revelations 12:10 -- And I heard a loud voice saying in heaven, Now is come salvation, and strength, and the kingdom of our God, and the power of his Christ: for the accuser of our brethren is cast down, which accused them before our God day and night.

Revelations 2:26 -- And he that overcometh, and keepeth my works unto the end, to him will I give power over the nations:

Revelations 21:7 -- He that overcometh shall inherit all things; and I will be his God, and he shall be my son.

Revelations 12:11 -- And they overcame him by the blood of the Lamb, and by the word of their testimony; and they loved not their lives unto the death.

Romans 8:15 -- For ye have not received the spirit of bondage again to fear; but ye have received the Spirit of adoption, whereby we cry, Abba, Father.

Romans 8:26 -- Likewise the Spirit also helpeth our infirmities: for we know not what we should pray for as we ought: but the Spirit itself maketh intercession for us with groanings which cannot be uttered.

Watchfulness

Proverbs 8:34 -- Blessed is the man that heareth me, watching daily at my gates, waiting at the posts of my doors.

1 Peter 4:7 -- But the end of all things is at hand: be ye therefore sober, and watch unto prayer.

1 Thessalonians 5:6 -- Therefore let us not sleep, as do others; but let us watch and be sober.

2 Timothy 4:5 -- But watch thou in all things, endure afflictions, do the work of an evangelist, make full proof of thy ministry.

Colossians 4:2 -- Continue in prayer, and watch in the same with thanksgiving;

Ephesians 6:18 -- Praying always with all prayer and supplication in the Spirit, and watching thereunto with all perseverance and supplication for all saints;

Hebrews 13:7 -- Remember them which have the rule over you, who have spoken unto you the word of God: whose faith follow, considering the end of their conversation.

Mark 13:33-34 -- Take ye heed, watch and pray: for ye know not when the time is. For the Son of man is as a man taking a far journey, who left his house, and gave authority to his servants, and to every man his work, and commanded the porter to watch.

Mark 14:38 -- Watch ye and pray, lest ye enter into temptation. The spirit truly is ready, but the flesh is weak.

Revelations 16:15 -- Behold, I come as a thief. Blessed is he that watcheth, and keepeth his garments, lest he walk naked, and they see his shame.

Revival

Habakkuk 3:2 -- O LORD, I have heard thy speech, and was afraid: O LORD, revive thy work in the midst of the years, in the midst of the years make known; in wrath remember mercy.

2 Corinthians 5:17 -- Therefore if any man be in Christ, he is a new creature: old things are passed away; behold, all things are become new.

Colossians 3:2-4 -- Set your affection on things above, not on things on the earth. For ye are dead, and your life is hid with Christ in God. When Christ, who is our life, shall appear, then shall ye also appear with him in glory.

Exodus 31:3 -- And I have filled him with the spirit of God, in wisdom, and in understanding, and in knowledge, and in all manner of workmanship,

Habakkuk 3:2-3 -- O LORD, I have heard thy speech, and was afraid: O LORD, revive thy work in the midst of the years, in the midst of the years make known; in wrath remember mercy. God came from Teman, and the Holy One from mount Paran. Selah. His glory covered the heavens, and the earth was full of his praise.

Hosea 6:2 -- After two days will he revive us: in the third day he will raise us up, and we shall live in his sight.

Hosea 10:12 -- Sow to yourselves in righteousness, reap in mercy; break up your fallow ground: for it is time to seek the LORD, till he come and rain righteousness upon you.

Hosea 14:7 -- They that dwell under his shadow shall return; they shall revive as the corn, and grow as the vine: the scent thereof shall be as the wine of Lebanon.

Isaiah 57:15 -- For thus saith the high and lofty One that inhabiteth eternity, whose name is Holy; I dwell in the high and holy place, with him also that is of a contrite and humble spirit, to revive the spirit of the humble, and to revive the heart of the contrite ones.

Isaiah 58:8 -- Then shall thy light break forth as the morning, and thine health shall spring forth speedily: and thy righteousness shall go before thee; the glory of the LORD shall be thy rereward.

Isaiah 64:1-3 -- Oh that thou wouldest rend the heavens, that thou wouldest come down, that the mountains might flow down at thy presence, As when the melting fire burneth, the fire causeth the waters to boil, to make thy name known to thine adversaries, that the nations may tremble at thy presence! When thou didst terrible things which we looked not for, thou camest down, the mountains flowed down at thy presence.

John 4:24 -- God is a Spirit: and they that worship him must worship him in spirit and in truth.

Luke 1:78 -- Through the tender mercy of our God; whereby the dayspring from on high hath visited us,

Matthew 5:6 -- Blessed are they which do hunger and thirst after righteousness: for they shall be filled.

Philippians 4:5 -- Let your moderation be known unto all men. The Lord is at hand.

Psalm 138:7 -- Though I walk in the midst of trouble, thou wilt revive me: thou shalt stretch forth thine hand against the wrath of mine enemies, and thy right hand shall save me.

Psalm 27:8-9 -- When thou saidst, Seek ye my face; my heart said unto thee, Thy face, LORD, will I seek. Hide not thy face far from me; put not thy servant away in anger: thou hast been my help; leave me not, neither forsake me, O God of my salvation.

Psalm 42:1 -- To the chief Musician, Maschil, for the sons of Korah. As the hart panteth after the water brooks, so panteth my soul after thee, O God.

Psalm 85:6 -- Wilt thou not revive us again: that thy people may rejoice in thee?

Unity
Psalm 133:1 -- A Song of degrees of David. Behold, how good and how pleasant it is for brethren to dwell together in unity!

1 Corinthians 12:12 -- For as the body is one, and hath many members, and all the members of that one body, being many, are one body: so also is Christ.

1 Corinthians 6:19 -- What? know ye not that your body is the temple of the Holy Ghost which is in you, which ye have of God, and ye are not your own?

Acts 2:1 -- And when the day of Pentecost was fully come, they were all with one accord in one place.

Acts 5:12 -- And by the hands of the apostles were many signs and wonders wrought among the people; (and they were all with one accord in Solomon's porch.

Acts 8:6 -- And the people with one accord gave heed unto those things which Philip spake, hearing and seeing the miracles which he did.

Amos 3:3 -- Can two walk together, except they be agreed?

Colossians 3:14 -- And above all these things put on charity, which is the bond of perfectness.

Ephesians 4:13 -- Till we all come in the unity of the faith, and of the knowledge of the Son of God, unto a perfect man, unto the measure of the stature of the fulness of Christ:

Ephesians 4:2-3 -- With all lowliness and meekness, with longsuffering, forbearing one another in love; Endeavouring to keep the unity of the Spirit in the bond of peace.

Ephesians 4:32 -- And be ye kind one to another, tenderhearted, forgiving one another, even as God for Christ's sake hath forgiven you.

Ephesians 4:4 -- There is one body, and one Spirit, even as ye are called in one hope of your calling;

Mark 10:9 -- What therefore God hath joined together, let not man put asunder.

Philippians 2:2 -- Fulfil ye my joy, that ye be likeminded, having the same love, being of one accord, of one mind.

Church Growth

Acts 2:42-47 -- *And they continued stedfastly in the apostles' doctrine and fellowship, and in breaking of bread, and in prayers. And fear came upon every soul: and many wonders and signs were done by the apostles. And all that believed were together, and had all things common; And sold their possessions and goods, and parted them to all men, as every man had need. And they, continuing daily with one accord in the temple, and breaking bread from house to house, did eat their meat with gladness and singleness of heart, Praising God, and having favour with all the people. And the Lord added to the church daily such as should be saved.*

1 Corinthians 12:28 -- And God hath set some in the church, first apostles, secondarily prophets, thirdly teachers, after that miracles, then gifts of healings, helps, governments, diversities of tongues.

1 Corinthians 14:12 -- Even so ye, forasmuch as ye are zealous of spiritual gifts, seek that ye may excel to the edifying of the church.

2 Timothy 2:2 -- And the things that thou hast heard of me among many witnesses, the same commit thou to faithful men, who shall be able to teach others also.

Acts 16:5 -- And so were the churches established in the faith, and increased in number daily.

Acts 20:28 -- Take heed therefore unto yourselves, and to all the flock, over the which the Holy Ghost hath made you overseers, to feed the church of God, which he hath purchased with his own blood.

Hebrews 10:25 -- Not forsaking the assembling of ourselves together, as the manner of some is; but exhorting one another: and so much the more, as ye see the day approaching.

James 5:14 -- Is any sick among you? let him call for the elders of the church; and let them pray over him, anointing him with oil in the name of the Lord:

Nations

Psalm 2:8 -- *Ask of me, and I shall give thee the heathen for thine inheritance, and the uttermost parts of the earth for thy possession.*

1 Timothy 2:1-2 -- I exhort therefore, that, first of all, supplications, prayers, intercessions, and giving of thanks, be made for all men; For kings, and for all that are in authority; that we may lead a quiet and peaceable life in all godliness and honesty.

2 Chronicles 20:6 -- And said, O LORD God of our fathers, art not thou God in heaven? and rulest not thou over all the kingdoms of the heathen? and in thine hand is there not power and might, so that none is able to withstand thee?

2 Chronicles 7:14 -- If my people, which are called by my name, shall humble themselves, and pray, and seek my face, and turn from their wicked ways; then will I hear from heaven, and will forgive their sin, and will heal their land.

Deuteronomy 14:2 -- For thou art an holy people unto the LORD thy God, and the LORD hath chosen thee to be a peculiar people unto himself, above all the nations that are upon the earth.

Ezekiel 34:28 -- And they shall no more be a prey to the heathen, neither shall the beast of the land devour them; but they shall dwell safely, and none shall make them afraid.

Isaiah 11:9 -- They shall not hurt nor destroy in all my holy mountain: for the earth shall be full of the knowledge of the LORD, as the waters cover the sea.

Matthew 28:19 -- Go ye therefore, and teach all nations, baptizing them in the name of the Father, and of the Son, and of the Holy Ghost:

Proverbs 2:21-22 -- For the upright shall dwell in the land, and the perfect shall remain in it. But the wicked shall be cut off from the earth, and the transgressors shall be rooted out of it.

Proverbs 16:10 -- A divine sentence is in the lips of the king: his mouth transgresseth not in judgment.

Proverbs 16:12-13 -- It is an abomination to kings to commit wickedness: for the throne is established by righteousness. Righteous lips are the delight of kings; and they love him that speaketh right.

Proverbs 20:28 -- Mercy and truth preserve the king: and his throne is upholden by mercy.

Proverbs 28:2 -- For the transgression of a land many are the princes thereof: but by a man of understanding and knowledge the state thereof shall be prolonged.

Proverbs 29:2 -- When the righteous are in authority, the people rejoice: but when the wicked beareth rule, the people mourn.

Romans 10:14 -- How then shall they call on him in whom they have not believed? and how shall they believe in him of whom they have not heard? and how shall they hear without a preacher?

Romans 10:15 -- And how shall they preach, except they be sent? as it is written, How beautiful are the feet of them that preach the gospel of peace, and bring glad tidings of good things!

Leaders & Those in Authority

1 Timothy 2:1-3 -- *I exhort therefore, that, first of all, supplications, prayers, intercessions, and giving of thanks, be made for all men; For kings, and for all that are in authority; that we may lead a quiet and peaceable life in all godliness and honesty. For this is good and acceptable in the sight of God our Saviour;*

1 Corinthians 12:28 -- And God hath set some in the church, first apostles, secondarily prophets, thirdly teachers, after that miracles, then gifts of healings, helps, governments, diversities of tongues.

1 Corinthians 12:8 -- For to one is given by the Spirit the word of wisdom; to another the word of knowledge by the same Spirit;

1 Peter 2:14 -- Or unto governors, as unto them that are sent by him for the punishment of evildoers, and for the praise of them that do well.

1 Peter 4:11 -- If any man speak, let him speak as the oracles of God; if any man minister, let him do it as of the ability which God giveth: that God in all things may be glorified through Jesus Christ, to whom be praise and dominion for ever and ever. Amen.

1 Timothy 2:2 -- For kings, and for all that are in authority; that we may lead a quiet and peaceable life in all godliness and honesty.

2 Chronicles 15:7 -- Be ye strong therefore, and let not your hands be weak: for your work shall be rewarded.

2 Corinthians 2:14 -- Now thanks be unto God, which always causeth us to triumph in Christ, and maketh manifest the savour of his knowledge by us in every place.

2 Corinthians 3:2-3 -- Ye are our epistle written in our hearts, known and read of all men: Forasmuch as ye are manifestly declared to be the epistle of Christ ministered by us, written not with ink, but with the Spirit of the living God; not in tables of stone, but in fleshy tables of the heart.

2 Corinthians 3:17 -- Now the Lord is that Spirit: and where the Spirit of the Lord is, there is liberty.

2 Corinthians 6:3-4 -- Giving no offence in any thing, that the ministry be not blamed: But in all things approving ourselves as the ministers of God, in much patience, in afflictions, in necessities, in distresses,

2 Corinthians 9:8 -- And God is able to make all grace abound toward you; that ye, always having all sufficiency in all things, may abound to every good work:

Deuteronomy 28:10 -- And all people of the earth shall see that thou art called by the name of the LORD; and they shall be afraid of thee.

Ephesians 3:20 -- Now unto him that is able to do exceeding abundantly above all that we ask or think, according to the power that worketh in us,

Isaiah 35:3 -- Strengthen ye the weak hands, and confirm the feeble knees.

Isaiah 40:11 -- He shall feed his flock like a shepherd: he shall gather the lambs with his arm, and carry them in his bosom, and shall gently lead those that are with young.

Jeremiah 23:4 -- And I will set up shepherds over them which shall feed them: and they shall fear no more, nor be dismayed, neither shall they be lacking, saith the LORD.

Proverbs 21:1 -- The king's heart is in the hand of the LORD, as the rivers of water: he turneth it whithersoever he will.

Psalm 33:12 -- Blessed is the nation whose God is the LORD; and the people whom he hath chosen for his own inheritance.

Psalm 67:4 -- O let the nations be glad and sing for joy: for thou shalt judge the people righteously, and govern the nations upon earth. Selah.

Romans 13:1 -- Let every soul be subject unto the higher powers. For there is no power but of God: the powers that be are ordained of God.

Romans 13:3 -- For rulers are not a terror to good works, but to the evil. Wilt thou then not be afraid of the power? do that which is good, and thou shalt have praise of the same:

Missions
2 Corinthians 2:14 -- *Now thanks be unto God, which always causeth us to triumph in Christ, and maketh manifest the savour of his knowledge by us in every place.*

1 Corinthians 12:8 -- For to one is given by the Spirit the word of wisdom; to another the word of knowledge by the same Spirit;

1 Peter 4:11 -- If any man speak, let him speak as the oracles of God; if any man minister, let him do it as of the ability which God giveth: that God in all things may be glorified through Jesus Christ, to whom be praise and dominion for ever and ever. Amen.

2 Chronicles 15:7 -- Be ye strong therefore, and let not your hands be weak: for your work shall be rewarded.

2 Corinthians 2:17 -- For we are not as many, which corrupt the word of God: but as of sincerity, but as of God, in the sight of God speak we in Christ.

2 Corinthians 3:17 -- Now the Lord is that Spirit: and where the Spirit of the Lord is, there is liberty.

2 Corinthians 3:2-3 -- Ye are our epistle written in our hearts, known and read of all men: Forasmuch as ye are manifestly declared to be the epistle of Christ ministered by us, written not with ink, but with the Spirit of the living God; not in tables of stone, but in fleshy tables of the heart.

2 Corinthians 6:3-4 -- Giving no offence in any thing, that the ministry be not blamed: But in all things approving ourselves as the ministers of God, in much patience, in afflictions, in necessities, in distresses,

2 Corinthians 9:8 -- And God is able to make all grace abound toward you; that ye, always having all sufficiency in all things, may abound to every good work:

2 Corinthians 12:9 -- And he said unto me, My grace is sufficient for thee: for my strength is made perfect in weakness. Most gladly therefore will I rather glory in my infirmities, that the power of Christ may rest upon me.

2 Thessalonians 3:3 -- But the Lord is faithful, who shall stablish you, and keep you from evil.

Acts 8:14 -- Now when the apostles which were at Jerusalem heard that Samaria had received the word of God, they sent unto them Peter and John:

Acts 8:15 -- Who, when they were come down, prayed for them, that they might receive the Holy Ghost:

Acts 8:17 -- Then laid they their hands on them, and they received the Holy Ghost.

Acts 8:4 -- Therefore they that were scattered abroad went every where preaching the word.

Acts 8:6-8 -- And the people with one accord gave heed unto those things which Philip spake, hearing and seeing the miracles which he did. For unclean spirits, crying with loud voice, came out of many that were possessed with them: and many taken with palsies, and that were lame, were healed. And there was great joy in that city.

Acts 11:21 -- And the hand of the Lord was with them: and a great number believed, and turned unto the Lord.

Habakkuk 3:19 -- The LORD God is my strength, and he will make my feet like hinds' feet, and he will make me to walk upon mine high places. To the chief singer on my stringed instruments.

Isaiah 40:11 -- He shall feed his flock like a shepherd: he shall gather the lambs with his arm, and carry them in his bosom, and shall gently lead those that are with young.

Isaiah 41:10 -- Fear thou not; for I am with thee: be not dismayed; for I am thy God: I will strengthen thee; yea, I will help thee; yea, I will uphold thee with the right hand of my righteousness.

Isaiah 54:17 -- No weapon that is formed against thee shall prosper; and every tongue that shall rise against thee in judgment thou shalt condemn. This is the heritage of the servants of the LORD, and their righteousness is of me, saith the LORD.

Isaiah 55:11-12 -- So shall my word be that goeth forth out of my mouth: it shall not return unto me void, but it shall accomplish that which I please, and it shall prosper in the thing whereto I sent it. For ye shall go out with joy, and be led forth with peace: the mountains and the hills shall break forth before you into singing, and all the trees of the field shall clap their hands.

Mark 16:15 -- And he said unto them, Go ye into all the world, and preach the gospel to every creature.

Matthew 18:18 -- Verily I say unto you, Whatsoever ye shall bind on earth shall be bound in heaven: and whatsoever ye shall loose on earth shall be loosed in heaven.

Psalm 2:8 -- Ask of me, and I shall give thee the heathen for thine inheritance, and the uttermost parts of the earth for thy possession.

Psalm 27:5 -- For in the time of trouble he shall hide me in his pavilion: in the secret of his tabernacle shall he hide me; he shall set me up upon a rock.

Psalm 146:7 -- Which executeth judgment for the oppressed: which giveth food to the hungry. The LORD looseth the prisoners:

The Unsaved

Ephesians 2:8 -- For by grace are ye saved through faith; and that not of yourselves: it is the gift of God:

2 Corinthians 4:4 -- In whom the god of this world hath blinded the minds of them which believe not, lest the light of the glorious gospel of Christ, who is the image of God, should shine unto them.

Acts 4:12 -- Neither is there salvation in any other: for there is none other name under heaven given among men, whereby we must be saved.

Galatians 3:13 -- Christ hath redeemed us from the curse of the law, being made a curse for us: for it is written, Cursed is every one that hangeth on a tree:

Psalm 25:5 -- Lead me in thy truth, and teach me: for thou art the God of my salvation; on thee do I wait all the day.

Psalm 106:4 -- Remember me, O LORD, with the favour that thou bearest unto thy people: O visit me with thy salvation;

Revelations 12:10 -- And I heard a loud voice saying in heaven, Now is come salvation, and strength, and the kingdom of our God, and the power of his Christ: for the accuser of our brethren is cast down, which accused them before our God day and night.

Romans 10:1 -- Brethren, my heart's desire and prayer to God for Israel is, that they might be saved.

Romans 10:17 -- So then faith cometh by hearing, and hearing by the word of God.

Romans 6:23 -- For the wages of sin is death; but the gift of God is eternal life through Jesus Christ our Lord.

The Backslidden

Hosea 14:4 -- *I will heal their backsliding, I will love them freely: for mine anger is turned away from him.*

Colossians 1:21-23 -- And you, that were sometime alienated and enemies in your mind by wicked works, yet now hath he reconciled in the body of his flesh through death, to present you holy and unblameable and unreproveable in his sight: If ye continue in the faith grounded and settled, and be not moved away from the hope of the gospel, which ye have heard, and which was preached to every creature which is under heaven; whereof I Paul am made a minister;

Galatians 6:1 -- Brethren, if a man be overtaken in a fault, ye which are spiritual, restore such an one in the spirit of meekness; considering thyself, lest thou also be tempted.

Hosea 5:15 -- I will go and return to my place, till they acknowledge their offence, and seek my face: in their affliction they will seek me early.

Isaiah 26:3 -- Thou wilt keep him in perfect peace, whose mind is stayed on thee: because he trusteth in thee.

Jeremiah 3:14 -- Turn, O backsliding children, saith the LORD; for I am married unto you: and I will take you one of a city, and two of a family, and I will bring you to Zion:

Psalm 103:3 -- Who forgiveth all thine iniquities; who healeth all thy diseases;

Psalm 37:24 -- Though he fall, he shall not be utterly cast down: for the LORD upholdeth him with his hand.

Psalm 85:8 -- I will hear what God the LORD will speak: for he will speak peace unto his people, and to his saints: but let them not turn again to folly.

False Accusation
Psalm 91:4-5 -- *He shall cover thee with his feathers, and under his wings shalt thou trust: his truth shall be thy shield and buckler.*

Slander
Matthew 12:36 -- *But I say unto you, That every idle word that men shall speak, they shall give account thereof in the day of judgment.*

1 Peter 3:16 -- Having a good conscience; that, whereas they speak evil of you, as of evildoers, they may be ashamed that falsely accuse your good conversation in Christ.

2 Timothy 4:17 -- Notwithstanding the Lord stood with me, and strengthened me; that by me the preaching might be fully known, and that all the Gentiles might hear: and I was delivered out of the mouth of the lion.

Ephesians 4:31 -- Let all bitterness, and wrath, and anger, and clamour, and evil speaking, be put away from you, with all malice:

Isaiah 41:10 -- Fear thou not; for I am with thee: be not dismayed; for I am thy God: I will strengthen thee; yea, I will help thee; yea, I will uphold thee with the right hand of my righteousness.

Isaiah 44:11 -- Behold, all his fellows shall be ashamed: and the workmen, they are of men: let them all be gathered together, let them stand up; yet they shall fear, and they shall be ashamed together.

Isaiah 50:7 -- For the Lord GOD will help me; therefore shall I not be confounded: therefore have I set my face like a flint, and I know that I shall not be ashamed.

Isaiah 50:9 -- Behold, the Lord GOD will help me; who is he that shall condemn me? lo, they all shall wax old as a garment; the moth shall eat them up.

Psalm 27:12 -- Deliver me not over unto the will of mine enemies: for false witnesses are risen up against me, and such as breathe out cruelty.

Psalm 31:13-16 -- For I have heard the slander of many: fear was on every side: while they took counsel together against me, they devised to take away my life. But I trusted in thee, O LORD: I said, Thou art my God.

My times are in thy hand: deliver me from the hand of mine enemies, and from them that persecute me. Make thy face to shine upon thy servant: save me for thy mercies' sake.

Psalm 34:13 -- Keep thy tongue from evil, and thy lips from speaking guile.

Psalm 35:11 -- False witnesses did rise up; they laid to my charge things that I knew not.

Psalm 35:19 -- Let not them that are mine enemies wrongfully rejoice over me: neither let them wink with the eye that hate me without a cause.

Psalm 35:23 -- Stir up thyself, and awake to my judgment, even unto my cause, my God and my Lord.

Psalm 35:26 -- Let them be ashamed and brought to confusion together that rejoice at mine hurt: let them be clothed with shame and dishonour that magnify themselves against me.

Psalm 38:13-15 -- But I, as a deaf man, heard not; and I was as a dumb man that openeth not his mouth. Thus I was as a man that heareth not, and in whose mouth are no reproofs. For in thee, O LORD, do I hope: thou wilt hear, O Lord my God.

Psalm 41:11-12 -- By this I know that thou favourest me, because mine enemy doth not triumph over me. And as for me, thou upholdest me in mine integrity, and settest me before thy face for ever.

Psalm 119:133 -- Order my steps in thy word: and let not any iniquity have dominion over me.

Romans 14:19 -- Let us therefore follow after the things which make for peace, and things wherewith one may edify another.

Titus 3:1-2 -- Put them in mind to be subject to principalities and powers, to obey magistrates, to be ready to every good work, to speak evil of no man, to be no brawlers, but gentle, shewing all meekness unto all men.

People in Crisis

Isaiah 50:4 -- *The Lord GOD hath given me the tongue of the learned, that I should know how to speak a word in season to him that is weary: he wakeneth morning by morning, he wakeneth mine ear to hear as the learned.*

2 Samuel 22:3 -- *The God of my rock; in him will I trust: he is my shield, and the horn of my salvation, my high tower, and my refuge, my saviour; thou savest me from violence.*

1 Peter 3:8 -- Finally, be ye all of one mind, having compassion one of another, love as brethren, be pitiful, be courteous:

2 Corinthians 1:3 -- Blessed be God, even the Father of our Lord Jesus Christ, the Father of mercies, and the God of all comfort;

2 Samuel 22:31 -- As for God, his way is perfect; the word of the LORD is tried: he is a buckler to all them that trust in him.

2 Timothy 1:12 -- For the which cause I also suffer these things: nevertheless I am not ashamed: for I know whom I have believed, and am persuaded that he is able to keep that which I have committed unto him against that day.

2 Timothy 1:7 -- For God hath not given us the spirit of fear; but of power, and of love, and of a sound mind.

Acts 20:35 -- I have shewed you all things, how that so labouring ye ought to support the weak, and to remember the words of the Lord Jesus, how he said, It is more blessed to give than to receive.

Deuteronomy 10:18 -- He doth execute the judgment of the fatherless and widow, and loveth the stranger, in giving him food and raiment.

Galatians 6:2 -- Bear ye one another's burdens, and so fulfil the law of Christ.

Hebrews 13:16 -- But to do good and to communicate forget not: for with such sacrifices God is well pleased.

Hebrews 13:3 -- Remember them that are in bonds, as bound with them; and them which suffer adversity, as being yourselves also in the body.

James 2:8 -- If ye fulfil the royal law according to the scripture, Thou shalt love thy neighbour as thyself, ye do well:

John 13:35 -- By this shall all men know that ye are my disciples, if ye have love one to another.

Matthew 25:34 -- Then shall the King say unto them on his right hand, Come, ye blessed of my Father, inherit the kingdom prepared for you from the foundation of the world:

Matthew 7:12 -- Therefore all things whatsoever ye would that men should do to you, do ye even so to them: for this is the law and the prophets.

Romans 12:15 -- Rejoice with them that do rejoice, and weep with them that weep.

Romans 15:1 -- We then that are strong ought to bear the infirmities of the weak, and not to please ourselves.

Deuteronomy 33:28 -- Israel then shall dwell in safety alone: the fountain of Jacob shall be upon a land of corn and wine; also his heavens shall drop down dew.

Isaiah 43:2 -- When thou passest through the waters, I will be with thee; and through the rivers, they shall not overflow thee: when thou walkest through the fire, thou shalt not be burned; neither shall the flame kindle upon thee.

Judges 18:10 -- When ye go, ye shall come unto a people secure, and to a large land: for God hath given it into your hands; a place where there is no want of any thing that is in the earth.

Job 11:18 -- And thou shalt be secure, because there is hope; yea, thou shalt dig about thee, and thou shalt take thy rest in safety.

Judges 1:24 -- Now unto him that is able to keep you from falling, and to present you faultless before the presence of his glory with exceeding joy,

Leviticus 25:18 -- Wherefore ye shall do my statutes, and keep my judgments, and do them; and ye shall dwell in the land in safety.

Leviticus 25:19 -- And the land shall yield her fruit, and ye shall eat your fill, and dwell therein in safety.

Leviticus 26:5-6 -- And your threshing shall reach unto the vintage, and the vintage shall reach unto the sowing time: and ye shall eat your bread to the full, and dwell in your land safely. And I will give peace in the land, and ye shall lie down, and none shall make you afraid: and I will rid evil beasts out of the land, neither shall the sword go through your land.

Luke 21:18 -- But there shall not an hair of your head perish.

Proverbs 11:14 -- Where no counsel is, the people fall: but in the multitude of counsellors there is safety.

Proverbs 11:21 -- Though hand join in hand, the wicked shall not be unpunished: but the seed of the righteous shall be delivered.

Proverbs 18:10 -- The name of the LORD is a strong tower: the righteous runneth into it, and is safe.

Proverbs 29:25 -- The fear of man bringeth a snare: but whoso putteth his trust in the LORD shall be safe. Luke 15:27

Proverbs 3:24 -- When thou liest down, thou shalt not be afraid: yea, thou shalt lie down, and thy sleep shall be sweet.

Proverbs 3:29 -- Devise not evil against thy neighbour, seeing he dwelleth securely by thee.

Psalm 12:5 -- For the oppression of the poor, for the sighing of the needy, now will I arise, saith the LORD; I will set him in safety from him that puffeth at him.

Psalm 3:3 -- But thou, O LORD, art a shield for me; my glory, and the lifter up of mine head.

Psalm 32:6-7 -- For this shall every one that is godly pray unto thee in a time when thou mayest be found: surely in the floods of great waters they shall not come nigh unto him. Thou art my hiding place; thou shalt preserve me from trouble; thou shalt compass me about with songs of deliverance. Selah.

Psalm 34:7 -- The angel of the LORD encampeth round about them that fear him, and delivereth them.

Psalm 46:1-2 -- To the chief Musician for the sons of Korah, A Song upon Alamoth. God is our refuge and strength, a very present help in trouble. Therefore will not we fear, though the earth be removed, and though the mountains be carried into the midst of the sea;

Psalm 91:15 -- He shall call upon me, and I will answer him: I will be with him in trouble; I will deliver him, and honour him.

Psalm 91:9-10 -- Because thou hast made the LORD, which is my refuge, even the most High, thy habitation; There shall no evil befall thee, neither shall any plague come nigh thy dwelling.

Psalm 94:22 -- But the LORD is my defence; and my God is the rock of my refuge.

Psalm 119:117 -- Hold thou me up, and I shall be safe: and I will have respect unto thy statutes continually.

Zechariah 2:5 -- For I, saith the LORD, will be unto her a wall of fire round about, and will be the glory in the midst of her.

The Bereaved
2 Corinthians 1:4 -- *Who comforteth us in all our tribulation, that we may be able to comfort them which are in any trouble, by the comfort wherewith we ourselves are comforted of God.*

    2 Thessalonians 2:16 -- Now our Lord Jesus Christ himself, and God, even our Father, which hath loved us, and hath given us everlasting consolation and good hope through grace,
    Hebrews 4:16 -- Let us therefore come boldly unto the throne of grace, that we may obtain mercy, and find grace to help in time of need.
    Isaiah 61:3 -- To appoint unto them that mourn in Zion, to give unto them beauty for ashes, the oil of joy for mourning, the garment of praise for the spirit of heaviness; that they might be called trees of righteousness, the planting of the LORD, that he might be glorified.
    Luke 4:18 -- The Spirit of the Lord is upon me, because he hath anointed me to preach the gospel to the poor; he hath sent me to heal the brokenhearted, to preach deliverance to the captives, and recovering of sight to the blind, to set at liberty them that are bruised,
    Matthew 5:4 -- Blessed are they that mourn: for they shall be comforted.

Hospitalized
James 5:13-16 -- *Is any among you afflicted? let him pray. Is any merry? let him sing Psalm. Is any sick among you? let him call for the elders of the church; and let them pray over him, anointing him with oil in the name of the Lord: And the prayer of faith shall save the sick, and the Lord shall raise him up; and if he have committed sins, they shall be forgiven him. Confess your faults one to another, and pray one for another, that ye may be healed.*
The effectual fervent prayer of a righteous man availeth much.

    1 Peter 2:24 -- Who his own self bare our sins in his own body on the tree, that we, being dead to sins, should live unto righteousness: by whose stripes ye were healed.
    3 John 1:2 -- Beloved, I wish above all things that thou mayest prosper and be in health, even as thy soul prospereth.

Deuteronomy 7:15 -- And the LORD will take away from thee all sickness, and will put none of the evil diseases of Egypt, which thou knowest, upon thee; but will lay them upon all them that hate thee.

Isaiah 53:4-5 -- Surely he hath borne our griefs, and carried our sorrows: yet we did esteem him stricken, smitten of God, and afflicted. But he was wounded for our transgressions, he was bruised for our iniquities: the chastisement of our peace was upon him; and with his stripes we are healed.

Job 37:23 -- Touching the Almighty, we cannot find him out: he is excellent in power, and in judgment, and in plenty of justice: he will not afflict.

Malachi 4:2 -- But unto you that fear my name shall the Sun of righteousness arise with healing in his wings; and ye shall go forth, and grow up as calves of the stall.

Matthew 8:7 -- And Jesus saith unto him, I will come and heal him.

Psalm 103:2-3 -- Bless the LORD, O my soul, and forget not all his benefits: Who forgiveth all thine iniquities; who healeth all thy diseases;

Psalm 107:20 -- He sent his word, and healed them, and delivered them from their destructions.

Psalm 91:10-12 -- There shall no evil befall thee, neither shall any plague come nigh thy dwelling. For he shall give his angels charge over thee, to keep thee in all thy ways. They shall bear thee up in their hands, lest thou dash thy foot against a stone.

Psalm 91:15-16 -- He shall call upon me, and I will answer him: I will be with him in trouble; I will deliver him, and honour him. With long life will I satisfy him, and shew him my salvation.

Legal Matters

Luke 12:11-12 -- *And when they bring you unto the synagogues, and unto magistrates, and powers, take ye no thought how or what thing ye shall answer, or what ye shall say: For the Holy Ghost shall teach you in the same hour what ye ought to say.*

1 Corinthians 1:8 -- Who shall also confirm you unto the end, that ye may be blameless in the day of our Lord Jesus Christ.

2 Timothy 1:7 -- For God hath not given us the spirit of fear; but of power, and of love, and of a sound mind.

Colossians 4:6 -- Let your speech be alway with grace, seasoned with salt, that ye may know how ye ought to answer every man.

Ephesians 6:10 -- Finally, my brethren, be strong in the Lord, and in the power of his might.

Ephesians 6:16 -- Above all, taking the shield of faith, wherewith ye shall be able to quench all the fiery darts of the wicked.

Isaiah 43:26 -- Put me in remembrance: let us plead together: declare thou, that thou mayest be justified.

Isaiah 49:25 -- But thus saith the LORD, Even the captives of the mighty shall be taken away, and the prey of the terrible shall be delivered: for I will contend with him that contendeth with thee, and I will save thy children.

Isaiah 54:14 -- In righteousness shalt thou be established: thou shalt be far from oppression; for thou shalt not fear: and from terror; for it shall not come near thee.

Isaiah 54:17 -- No weapon that is formed against thee shall prosper; and every tongue that shall rise against thee in judgment thou shalt condemn. This is the heritage of the servants of the LORD, and their righteousness is of me, saith the LORD.

Jeremiah 1:12 -- Then said the LORD unto me, Thou hast well seen: for I will hasten my word to perform it.

Jeremiah 33:3 -- Call unto me, and I will answer thee, and shew thee great and mighty things, which thou knowest not.

Luke 21:15 -- For I will give you a mouth and wisdom, which all your adversaries shall not be able to gainsay nor resist.

Matthew 18:18 -- Verily I say unto you, Whatsoever ye shall bind on earth shall be bound in heaven: and whatsoever ye shall loose on earth shall be loosed in heaven.

Proverbs 3:5-6 -- Trust in the LORD with all thine heart; and lean not unto thine own understanding. In all thy ways acknowledge him, and he shall direct thy paths.

Proverbs 14:25 -- A true witness delivereth souls: but a deceitful witness speaketh lies.

Evangelism

Isaiah 52:7 -- How beautiful upon the mountains are the feet of him that bringeth good tidings, that publisheth peace; that bringeth good tidings of good, that publisheth salvation; that saith unto Zion, Thy God reigneth!

Deuteronomy 32:3 -- Because I will publish the name of the LORD: ascribe ye greatness unto our God.

Habakkuk 2:2 -- And the LORD answered me, and said, Write the vision, and make it plain upon tables, that he may run that readeth it.

Habakkuk 2:3 -- For the vision is yet for an appointed time, but at the end it shall speak, and not lie: though it tarry, wait for it; because it will surely come, it will not tarry.

Mark 13:10 -- And the gospel must first be published among all nations.

Philippians 4:8 -- Finally, brethren, whatsoever things are true, whatsoever things are honest, whatsoever things are just, whatsoever things are pure, whatsoever things are lovely, whatsoever things are of good report; if there be any virtue, and if there be any praise, think on these things.

Proverbs 25:25 -- As cold waters to a thirsty soul, so is good news from a far country.

Psalm 26:7 -- That I may publish with the voice of thanksgiving, and tell of all thy wondrous works

Glossary

PRAY WHAT GOD SAYS
www.praywhatgodsays.info
Chrisbmar10@gmail.com
Blog: http://praywhatgodsays.posterous.com